"*Healing the Scars of Childhood Abuse* is a very important book. It takes on the lasting implications of childhood trauma with empathy and hope. Dr. Jantz tells the story of trauma through the eyes of the children. Those stories make this book a page-turner. As the stories unfold, the author's psychological wisdom and practical insight grow organically. In this way, this book is a moving personal experience. I highly recommend this book to anyone who is ready to heal the past and build a new future."

—**Michael Gurian**, *New York Times* bestselling author
of *The Wonder of Boys* and *The Wonder of Girls*

"*Healing the Scars of Childhood Abuse* by Dr. Jantz is a clearly written book that will be of great help to those dealing with the long-term effects of childhood abuse and wanting to heal and move on to deeper wholeness. I highly recommend it!"

—**Siang-Yang Tan, PhD**, professor of psychology,
Fuller Theological Seminary, and author of *Counseling
and Psychotherapy: A Christian Perspective*

"Dr. Jantz's counseling practice, speaking, and writing have brought hope to thousands. It's my prayer that thousands more will find healing and rest for their souls by reading this book—in particular, those struggling with the emotional and physical scars of childhood abuse. If you are struggling, then dive into this book like I did. You'll find insights into why the pain we experienced can make change so difficult. Even more, you'll find chapters full of hard-won knowledge and skills to break the cycle of hurt you've been in, pointing you toward a hopeful and blessed future—starting today."

—**John Trent, PhD**, Gary D. Chapman Chair of Marriage and
Family Ministry and Therapy, Moody Theological Seminary;
author of *The Blessing* and *LifeMapping*

Healing the Scars of Childhood Abuse

Books by Gregory L. Jantz, PhD,
with Ann McMurray

Healing the Scars of Emotional Abuse
Overcoming Anxiety, Worry, and Fear
Every Woman's Guide to Managing Your Anger

Books by Gregory L. Jantz, PhD,
and Dr. Tim Clinton with Ann McMurray

Don't Call It Love

Healing the Scars of Childhood Abuse

Moving beyond the Past
into a Healthy Future

Dr. Gregory L. Jantz, PhD
WITH ANN MCMURRAY

Revell

a division of Baker Publishing Group
Grand Rapids, Michigan

© 2017 by Gregory L. Jantz

Published by Revell
a division of Baker Publishing Group
P.O. Box 6287, Grand Rapids, MI 49516-6287
www.revellbooks.com

Printed in the United States of America

Library of Congress Cataloging-in-Publication Data is on file at the Library of Congress, Washington, DC.

ISBN 978-0-8007-2772-7

Scripture quotations are from the Holy Bible, New International Version®. NIV®. Copyright © 1973, 1978, 1984, 2011 by Biblica, Inc.™ Used by permission of Zondervan. All rights reserved worldwide. www.zondervan.com

This publication is intended to provide helpful and informative material on the subjects addressed. Readers should consult their personal health professionals before adopting any of the suggestions in this book or drawing inferences from it. The author and publisher expressly disclaim responsibility for any adverse effects arising from the use or application of the information contained in this book.

17 18 19 20 21 22 23   7 6 5 4 3 2 1

In keeping with biblical principles of creation stewardship, Baker Publishing Group advocates the responsible use of our natural resources. As a member of the Green Press Initiative, our company uses recycled paper when possible. The text paper of this book is composed in part of post-consumer waste.

This book is dedicated to Lonnie Hull DuPont. Her support over the years has been invaluable, as has her steadfast commitment to bringing hope through the written word at Revell. Thank you, Lonnie, for your tireless advocacy for the hurting, especially the children of abuse.

Contents

1. The Hide-and-Seek of Childhood Abuse   17

Childhood abuse takes on many faces—emotional, physical, sexual—through persistent patterns or a single traumatic event. Those who commit such shameful acts rarely accept any blame for those actions and instead seek to indict the innocent.

2. Not Normal but Too Common   27

Children, by nature, should be protected and nurtured by those older, stronger, and more powerful. Yet children often find themselves targeted in subservient positions, unprotected and at-risk.

3. The Cost of Survival   39

Abused children can become adept at finding ways to survive, born out of desperation and their incomplete understanding. Initially useful, these survival skills can begin to complicate and damage the path to mature adult functioning.

Acknowledgments

These pages reflect the work and passion of so many who partner with me at The Center • A Place of HOPE. I am surrounded by a team of true professionals, who, with God's help, are daily instruments of hope and healing. I also want to acknowledge Ann, whose faithfulness is done with joy and whose artistry is reflected in these pages.

Introduction

Finding Your Way Forward

Something dreadful happened on the way to adulthood for far too many children. Perhaps you're one of them. Perhaps the childhood you so desperately wanted didn't happen for you. Instead, your childhood wasn't something you dreamed about; your childhood was a nightmare you survived. And for some of you, just barely.

Childhood is supposed to be a loving, nurturing, and empowering time for children to be strengthened and supported into adulthood. When childhood abuse enters into that picture, that reality becomes torn and tattered. How do you find a way to pick up those fragments of your life and move forward?

As a professional therapist, I've heard that question asked in innumerable ways over the years. I've heard that question asked by women and men of different ages, beliefs, backgrounds, and economic circumstances. The question is, in many ways, a universal one.

While the question may be universal for those who have experienced childhood abuse, the answers are extremely personal. This book is written as a guide to understanding the challenges of overcoming childhood abuse, and I'll present information in a type of overview. However, this book is also written to help each reader reach back into their own childhood and then move forward for those personal answers that create healing and recovery.

As an author, I know I couldn't possibility write down all the answers. As a therapist, I know I don't have all the answers in the first place. What I do have, as an author and as a therapist, are the questions. I've known for years that I can't heal anyone. What I can do is help people understand the questions so they can find the answers to hopefully help ease the hurt in their lives.

Is the search for answers difficult? Yes, but people who reach the point of searching are already in pain. The pain, their own or the pain of their family and loved ones, is a powerful motivator to find the way forward—past the discomfort and into a more positive future.

I believe that while the past affects the future, the future need not be enslaved to the past. Yesterday cannot be changed, but tomorrow hasn't been written yet. Each new day brings the promise of hope. I've found in my own life, both personally and professionally, that hope is incredibly powerful. You will find great hope in asking questions, because behind every question lies the hope of an answer. As you read this book, discover your questions, search for your answers, and hang on to hope. Watch for hope to do amazing things.

1

The Hide-and-Seek of Childhood Abuse

Everyone knows there is no perfect family. No father is always loving and patient and engaged. No mother is always understanding and helpful and kind. No older sibling is always inclusive and attentive and affectionate. No younger sibling is always respectful and considerate and agreeable. Those who enter into a family do not always embrace all members of that family. Behind closed doors, people can and do act badly, make mistakes, and give in to their weaknesses. The perfect family, the perfect parent or sibling, the perfect childhood is an ephemeral dream that evaporates in the harsh light of human failings and unforeseen circumstances. Yet I have come to believe that the idea of perfect is still a compelling dream for children, and the adults they become. Children dream of a life where they are truly loved and cared for, and wish for that dream with all their might. When they are deprived of that dream, children mourn its loss, through frustration, disappointment, anger, regret, and tragically, blame and shame.

As they wish for and dream of the what-if perfect life, children learn to settle for something much less. Their lives may not be perfect, but what about normal? Normal makes you no better or no worse than everyone else. Normal means that when bad things happen to you, those are "just because" instead of "because of me." Normal protects against shame. Reaching for normal can take the target off your back. Considering your life, such as it is, to be "normal" can depersonalize the difficult.

A person can look back on a difficult childhood through a lens of normalcy. But when does normal stop being normal and become something else? When does that continuum of perfect-to-normal veer off into the realm of abuse? When does the pathway from everything you wish for plummet into everything you fear?

Children live in a world where their choices are made for them and power over their lives rests in the hands of adults. Within that state, what child wants to acknowledge a horrific childhood, with little hope and no end in sight? Isn't it better to use the one power children do have—the power of imagination—to pretend things aren't so bad?

"I kept running away from the truth that I wasn't loved," Judy admitted. "I guess, in a way, I've always been running away from it. Growing up, I didn't get what I so desperately wanted. Now, I never will. How do I accept that?"

Judy is like many people with a background of childhood abuse who I've encountered over my years of counseling. As an adult, Judy wanted to be able to claim a perfect childhood for herself, where she was loved and special and cared for. Intellectually, as an adult, she knew that hadn't happened. Emotionally, to cope with the loss, she settled for viewing her childhood as not great but, at least, normal. Judy's childhood, though, was not normal. Oh, she caught infrequent glimpses of what a normal childhood might look and feel like. These scraps of affection were enough to keep an emotionally starved child alive one more day, surviving on hopes and dreams and desperate wishes for more.

Do you remember, as a child, being trapped in some difficult or traumatic event and shutting your eyes and telling yourself that whatever it was would soon be over? As long as you didn't look at it or hear it or acknowledge it, the bad thing surely would go away. "Don't think about it," you would tell yourself. "Find a way to get beyond it, then pretend like it didn't happen." Children find such ways to survive difficult things. They tell themselves over and over again it isn't so bad. If there's no escaping the bad, then they pretend it isn't so bad. Admitting the bad just makes it more real.

Truth and Illusion

This book is about the torment of childhood abuse. Children, sadly, are abused in too many ways, from physical beatings to sexual exploitation to psychological torment. I have found children, and the adults they become, have similar ways to cope with the nightmare of their childhood abuse. Many camouflage their abusive past under the gloss of normalcy and the rationale of "it wasn't so bad." Others have no illusion about the wretched nature of their childhoods. They are quite aware that the verbal tirades or the beatings or the sexual abuse were not normal. Yet they still desperately seek to conceal their past from others under a shroud of normalcy. Some know their lives were not normal but consider themselves, not the actions of others, the source of the abnormality. They blame themselves and seek to hide their shame.

For children who have been abused, I have found hiding behind a curtain of normalcy is a way to survive the past. Stopping to really look at and accept the past as not normal can feel like experiencing a death—the death of the dream of "what should have been." When that dream is all you have to hold on to, why in the world would you want to let it go? Why exchange a comforting fantasy for a painful reality?

My hope is to answer those questions, to give you reasons to accept your past, abuse included. My hope is to provide you with a way to separate what parts of your life you can claim as normal and what parts of your life were not. And, most of all, my hope is to help you untangle shame and blame, what you knew growing up from who you are now. To paraphrase the Serenity Prayer, my hope is for you to accept the things about your childhood you cannot change, find the courage to change the things you can, and gain wisdom to know the difference so you can move forward with your life.

This wisdom to know the difference between truth and illusion is not easy to come by. If you've lived a great deal of your life under an illusion, how are you to see the truth? How do you go back and look at your life and decide where your experiences fit? What was truly normal? What was, sadly, abusive? And are you the only judge? What if you were never physically beaten or sexually exploited? When there are no welts or bruises or broken bones, no molestation or penetration, were you still abused? What about emotional abuse?

Societal norms add another layer to these questions. Back when you were growing up, "normal" looked different than it does now. For example, what used to be considered proper parental discipline in some circles is now acknowledged by many as physical abuse. Some sexual customs, once considered private and inviolate, are now viewed as sexually abusive and societally unacceptable. In the past, how a child was psychologically treated was considered irrelevant, as long as the child had a roof over their head, clothes on their body, and food to eat. Now, however, the psychological treatment and mistreatment of children is increasingly studied and given special importance.

What Is Childhood Abuse?

With lines shifting and cultural views changing, just what is childhood abuse? To understand what falls under this spectrum of childhood abuse, I have found it helpful to focus on not only the behaviors but also the effects of those behaviors. I believe childhood abuse is a systematic, persistent pattern of psychological, physical, and/or sexual behaviors that denigrate and devalue the identity and worth of a child. This childhood abuse shows itself in, I believe, four distinct and often interconnected ways—through emotional or psychological abuse, through physical abuse, through neglect, and through sexual abuse.

Childhood abuse is multilayered. Neglect and physical and sexual abuse are always accompanied by devastating emotional damage. This childhood abuse can appear as aggressive actions of harm as well as passive failures to act. Childhood abuse can manifest as a pattern of behavior over time but can also encompass a single severe and traumatic event that undermines a child's sense of self, immediate safety, and long-term security.

I will spend time going over various types of childhood abuse, the effects of such abuse, and ways to overcome and heal from abuse. But before I can do any of those things, I need to first deal with what I have seen as a significant barrier to healing from childhood abuse, which is this persistent clinging to the illusion of normalcy.

What about you? What was your normal? Perhaps your normal growing up was a house full of yelling, cursing, and chaos. You may have grown up routinely being slapped or kept from food or sleep. Your bedroom, when you were younger, may have been a place, not of dreams, but of nightmares. These situations were part of your normal life. You didn't like living like that, but you didn't know any other way. That life was normal for you and you found a way through it. You may have even felt pride that you survived and turned out as well as you did. Or you may, to this day, still experience deep shame regarding how you were treated and hide behind the curtain of normalcy. Regardless, you did what you had to and got by another day. Truthfully, the last thing you want to do now is go back and relive what you've been trying to put behind you.

Others of you, early on, understood your "special" status; you knew you weren't normal and believed you were to blame. You couldn't hide from the truth of your abuse; instead, your goal was to hide the truth of your abuse from others. You didn't want anyone to know how you were being treated because of the deep guilt and shame you felt. The horror of your abuse was always accompanied by the terror of someone discovering your humiliation and degradation. Deep down, you believed you were at fault. Either you deserved what happened to you or you were too weak to stop it. If others found out, they would blame you too and do nothing to protect you. You pretended to be normal to hide the truth you weren't.

If this is how you've dealt with the pain of your past, this illusion of normal may have become so engrained that it has taken on a life of its own. The illusion seems much easier to deal with than the truth. You may be trying to live your life completely in the present, avoiding any mention of your past, beyond the façade of normalcy you've hidden behind for years.

Bringing the Past to the Present

Going back and dealing with your past may not be what you want to do, but I firmly believe it is what you need to do. Words that bite and scratch and dig deep into the soul leave scars. Neglect and abandonment create holes of deprivation that resist being filled. Being used for the sexual gratification of others steals away identity and worth. Physical, sexual, and psychological wounds leave scars, whether hidden or acknowledged.

Rick looked back on his childhood as pretty normal. He lived in a normal house, in a normal neighborhood. Sure, his dad would periodically take a belt to his backside when he was younger, but he considered that normal. However, Rick told me he could barely sit after these sessions. He talked about how he tried to use his hands to shield the pain until his father started tying his wrists to a bedpost. When I asked Rick if his father said anything during these beatings, Rick explained that he would punctuate each blow with a verbal assault. Rick told me his father made sure he knew just why he deserved such punishment. When I asked if anyone in the house ever came to his aid, Rick admitted that sometimes his father seemed unable to stop the beatings until Rick's screams brought his mother's reluctant intervention. When he got older, Rick said the beatings ended but the verbal assaults did not. Rick didn't consider the verbal assaults abusive because he was no longer being physically beaten, but the bruising just moved from the outside to the inside.

Rick told me that was just the way the old man was. He learned to live with it back then and said he thought he'd put that past behind him. Then the panic attacks started and threatened to undo everything Rick had done to make up for his past. Rick came for help to overcome the panic attacks, not realizing the key to his present problem could only be found in his past.

Diane considered her childhood pretty normal. She wasn't one of the popular kids growing up, she admitted to me, but quickly added that neither were any of her friends. She said she never wanted to be popular, but she wasn't a "bad" kid either. Being bad or popular, Diane said, got you noticed at school, which wasn't good. Getting noticed made you a target, and the last thing Diane wanted at school was to be a target. She got enough of that at home.

Diane confessed she often found herself the focus of her mother's discontent, which could manifest at any time for obscure reasons. Diane was still confused about what would set her mother off. She tried to learn to be compliant, doing what she was told as quickly and as quietly as possible, to try to please her mother. "Flying under the radar" was how she put it. Diane told me, at some point, she gave up on receiving any kind of praise from her mother. The new standard Diane said she settled for was not to draw her mother's attention.

Diane thought she'd put the past behind her but admitted she was becoming angrier at living her life devoted to drawing no attention to herself. She had already quit two jobs in the past three years because she secretly fumed over how unfairly she'd been treated. Instead of saying anything and drawing attention to herself, she'd just quit. Diane quit those jobs, but she didn't quit thinking about those jobs and how unappreciated she'd been. Well into adulthood, Diane found herself mad, surprisingly furious, with no idea how to handle her rage.

Brent knew his life wasn't normal but did everything he could to hide that fact. Normal people, he said, were happy to see their grandparents. Not Brent. When Brent even looked at his grandfather, he got sick to his stomach and could feel an upwelling of that old, buried anger. Brent was angry that, even after what happened, his grandfather could still show up at the house, smiling and hugging all the grandkids. Brent said he never told his parents what had happened. He just shrugged when I asked him why not. What was he supposed to say? Besides, Brent said it had happened only twice during that summer he'd spent at his grandparents' house in Indiana. He was young and hadn't known what to do to escape. He assured me that when he was older, he made sure it never happened again.

Brent talked about how he went on with his life, distancing himself from his family the older he got. His grandfather got older too. Brent said he found it difficult to reconcile pictures of "that frail old man" with the one who had done those things so long ago. Brent said the way he handled it was just not to think about it, not talk about it. Above all else, he'd learned you don't trust; you don't let people close enough to hurt you. Then Brent started his own family.

Rick, Diane, and Brent all sought to view or present their childhood experiences through that illusion of normalcy. They could not understand why, with the past in the past, they were having so much difficulty navigating the present. Trying to keep the past pushed down wasn't working so well. Each realized they were trying to fit a "normal" shape around the jagged, hurtful edges of their experiences. Each had attempted over the years to outrun their past, moving on with life, careers, relationships, activities, family—going, doing, running. The past, however, kept seeping up, like thick, sticky tar, gumming up their best intentions in the present.

Childlike Faith

Rick, Diane, and Brent grew up because children do not stay children. As their worlds expanded, they came to realize the "normal" they experienced wasn't really the same as what others had experienced. The strategy of normalcy began to fray. What were they to do then? Stick with the façade of normalcy? Or come to accept a different kind of childhood? How is a person to accept the pain and shame that come from truly acknowledging an abusive childhood?

Everyone knows there is no such thing as a perfect family, but that doesn't stop a child from wanting one. Children have an incredibly powerful need to be loved, and they will hold on to that wish in the face of compelling evidence to the contrary. Why? Because children routinely believe in the impossible, mirrored in and fortified by childhood stories. In Disney's *Pinocchio*, Jiminy Cricket sings that "anything your heart desires will come to you." Lyrics like that and "when you wish upon a star, your dreams come true" promise children the power to change their worlds and do impossible things.

Children are dreamers. They are eternal optimists, as exemplified in the song "Tomorrow" from the musical *Annie*. In that song, an orphan, Annie, has a mantra for getting through difficult days by singing that the sun will come out tomorrow, while assuring herself that tomorrow is only a day away. Children have the capacity to believe in the sun, even when it is obscured by clouds. I believe this capacity to see clouds today but believe in the sun tomorrow empowers abused children to survive their abuse. The difficulty arises when illusion and truth, with clouds and sun, become confused and the child is no longer willing or able to differentiate one from the other.

In this book, I'm asking you to take a risk by acknowledging the clouds in your life. I'm asking you to open up that lockbox of "it wasn't so bad" and consider the possibility that it was. I'm asking you to open yourself up to accepting that what you experienced as a child was bad because it was wrong and painful. Moreover, I'm asking you to accept the truth, knowing acceptance will cause you more pain. And for those of you who are aware of the clouds you experienced as a child, I'm asking you to reach back, beyond the pain, humiliation, and devastation, to that child who still believed in the sun.

I'm asking you to hold on to faith. The faith I'm asking for, however, isn't found in the pages of a children's book but, rather, in a different sort of book. I'm asking you to reawaken your childlike faith, a faith that starts in childhood yet reaches beyond adulthood. This is the faith, Jesus said, with the power to unlock the kingdom of heaven.[1] I'm asking you to keep your faith in the impossible, even in the glare of reality's harsh light. You may not be able to find the way to impossible things, but "with God all things are possible."[2]

This book, then, is about the reality of our lives as emotional, relational, and physical beings and how childhood abuse affects that reality. However, this book is also about the truth of our lives as spiritual beings and how faith, hope, and love can make impossible dreams come true.

2

Not Normal but Too Common

God, she was tired. If she had to hear about one more problem, she swore she was going to explode. Pity the person who set her off; it wasn't going to be pretty. Nobody cared about her stress. All anybody cared about was what they needed, especially the kids. Give me this; I need that. The demands were endless. Her feet and back hurt. All she wanted was peace and quiet, which never seemed to happen with the TV blaring or that obnoxious soundtrack from her nine-year-old's latest video game, the one her ex bought him even though she had clearly said no.

The more Gayle thought about her life and her stresses, the madder she got. By the time she picked up the kids from after-school care, she was fuming. Both must have sensed how she was feeling, because they didn't say much as they got into the car. "Let's go," was all she said. That is, until Cameron got out that new game and started playing it before she even left the parking lot. That stupid, incessant music was the final straw—for the next ten minutes Gayle unloaded her anger, frustration, and resentment from the driver's seat to the back seat. Starting with her son, she outlined his disobedience from the previous week. Her daughter was hammered with the list of the things she'd done poorly or not at all. After arriving at home, both kids were sent to their rooms and the game taken away for a week. Gayle felt good that at least some things in her life were under her control.

Are you surprised that a scenario such as this would be in a book about childhood abuse? Did Gayle beat her kids physically? No. Did she use them for her own sexual gratification? No. Did she fail to feed or clothe them? No. Was Gayle abusive to her children? Yes. Gayle was emotionally abusive. She repeatedly blamed them for the problems in her life, over which they had no control and bore no responsibility. She had a terrible habit of punishing them for being children and, thus, deprived them of the joy in being children. She devised ways to use this blame and punishment of her children for personal emotional gratification, creating psychological, or emotional, abuse.

Children, by nature, should be protected and nurtured by those stronger and more powerful. Yet children can often find themselves in vulnerable, targeted positions. Childhood abuse is not normal, but, as a professional therapist, I find it distressingly common, especially when all types of childhood abuse are factored—physical abuse, neglect, sexual abuse, and, most common of all, emotional or psychological abuse.

Emotional Abuse

More than twenty years ago, I wrote a book on emotional abuse because I wasn't finding much acknowledgment regarding the damage I was seeing in my clients from emotional or psychological abuse. One question I asked in that book was why emotional abuse was so common. I concluded that emotional abuse was so prevalent because some people categorized emotional abuse as normal. How could something normal be considered abusive? So what if you were yelled at growing up, wasn't everyone? Who cared if you were regularly dismissed as worthless? You just needed to try harder. If you didn't grow up feeling loved, that was just a generational thing you were supposed to get over. If you weren't beaten within an inch of your life, you had nothing to complain about. So people didn't complain; they moved on with their lives. Yet some of those people kept having difficulties, difficulties that eventually led them to my office.

Do you remember the childhood story "The Emperor's New Clothes" by Hans Christian Andersen? In this story, two weavers promise a vain emperor a fine suit of clothes. However, these clothes could only be seen by those who were wise and knowledgeable. Those who were stupid or incompetent would be unfit to see the clothes. The weavers purport to have finished the clothing, mimic dressing the emperor, and then proceed to parade him about the village. The townspeople are afraid to be deemed unfit to see the splendid new clothes, so they ooh and aah and gush about the emperor's new clothes, that is, until a young child cries out that the emperor isn't wearing any. At that point, the bubble bursts and the adults in the crowd find the courage to admit the obvious.

People are slow to admit the obvious in cases of emotional abuse for various reasons. When I was growing up, years of groupthink said that adults, especially parents, had the right to deal with children however they saw fit. You weren't supposed to involve yourself in another family's "business." If adults spoke harshly to children, well, they must have had a reason. It wasn't your "place" to object—and certainly not in public.

My generation also grew up learning that "sticks and stones may break my bones but words will never hurt me." I remember repeating that rhyme to myself when other kids were mean to me. I learned the lesson well and determined I wasn't going to let other kids get to me. That rhyme wasn't as successful when it came to hurtful words from adults, and certainly not my parents. My father and mother still retained the power to hurt me with their words. Even my older sister could get under my guard with her words and her sometimes go-away attitude. Needless to say, I didn't grow up in a perfect family. I also didn't grow up in an abusive one. I grew up in a truly normal family, with parents who loved and cared for me, who gave me words of encouragement, and who sometimes hurt me with their words.

As far as I knew, the kids I hung out with growing up also lived in normal families, though the ratio of good-to-bad ran the gambit, from the house with what we used to call "the Kool-Aid mom" to the house with the dad who drank during the day. We didn't know any different. As kids, we roamed the neighborhood, reading the temperature of our block of houses, seeking out the best moods and best food. We didn't think about emotional abuse; we just knew the people and the houses to avoid. And we felt sorry for the kids who didn't have that option.

Growing up, about the only thing I could do for one of my buddies, who didn't have that option, was to let him have sleepovers at my house as much as possible. When the answer was no to sleeping over at my house, I'd find the courage to go to his house, hoping my being there would, in some way, keep him from being as much of a target. At that age, being his friend was my way of helping him.

As a kid, my buddy's life was his life and we found ways to work around the rough parts. One of those ways was for both of us to pretend the drunken tirades weren't so bad. My friend would make jokes about his dad and make-believe he didn't care; I'd laugh and let him.

My family moved and we lost touch, as kids often do. I've wondered, though, over the years, how he's doing with those rough parts of his life. To this day, I can still remember some of the terrible words his inebriated father would hurl in his direction. I've relived them in the lives and stories of those I've counseled. When I started my practice over thirty years ago, I committed to unclothe the lie that "words can never hurt." They can and they do, in stunning and devastating ways. When society collectively comes to that conclusion, the emotional abuse of children will become less common.

Physical Abuse

Emotional or psychological abuse underlies all other types of child-hood abuse. Sadly, children become not only verbal punching bags but also literal ones. As a society, we continue to wrestle with the lines between physical discipline of a child and physical abuse of a child. Most of us over a certain age grew up with spanking and slapping. If we misbehaved in school, we were possibly paddled as discipline. So, if a child can be hit by an adult in one situation, where is the line between discipline and abuse?

This debate was reignited several years ago, when a popular NFL player was indicted on charges of child abuse for hitting his four-year-old son with a wooden switch hard enough to cause welts. He pled no contest to child endangerment and spent part of a year suspended by the NFL but was reinstated after a court ruling overturned that suspension. People came to his defense, saying they had been similarly disciplined as children and turned out fine. Others, however, questioned the use of such discipline on a four-year-old. Some felt hitting a child with an open hand, such as spanking or slapping, was acceptable but hitting a child with a closed hand, a fist, or an object was not.

Others threw Proverbs 13:24 into the discussion. Growing up and going to church, I remember the shortened version of that proverb being, "Spare the rod, spoil the child." The full version is: "Whoever spares the rod hates their children, but the one who loves their children is careful to discipline them." Some questioned the definition of the word *discipline*, suggesting the root of that word is about teaching or instruction and does not refer to punishment. One person posited that the rod in question was a shepherd's crook (as in, "Thy rod and thy staff, they comfort me" from Psalm 23:4) used to guide and not to hit.[1] Defining childhood physical abuse in this one instance, with this one family, became a national conversation.

What about you? How do you define physical abuse of a child? Is your definition tied to what you experienced as a child yourself? Were you swatted, spanked, or "whooped" as a child? Were you hit, beaten, or kicked? Were you picked up, thrown against walls, knocked down stairs? Were you burned or scratched or cut? Were you too sore to move, sit, or walk afterward? And how did you feel about what happened? How did you feel about yourself? Was it your fault? Could you have made it better if only you'd tried harder to be good?

What was the reason for the physical actions against you? Were they to teach you a lesson? Were they because you were stupid or useless? Were they because the other person was tired or frustrated or angry or drunk or high? How often did they happen? Once in a blue moon? Once a month? Once a week? Once a day?

Some people believe spanking or swatting a child with an open hand is an effective way to gain that child's attention. If you believe that, is there a difference if that child is five or fifteen? Is it discipline to slap a child across the face once but physical abuse to do it again and again? Furthermore, is there a difference if the physical action is taken by a parent, a teacher, or a coach?

So many questions, and the answers do not find universal acceptance, as this case with the NFL player and his four-year-old son revealed. I answer the question of what is physically abusive the following way: physical abuse is the use of physical force to intentionally cause injury to a child, with that injury causing not only physical but also emotional damage.

A court may have overturned the player's suspension by the NFL, but the court of public opinion is still deliberating over the line between appropriate discipline and inappropriate and unacceptable physical abuse. In the case of your life and childhood, you will need to come to your own conclusions after a thorough look at your experiences and how those experiences were meant to make you feel. The lines are shifting, but until a widely accepted cultural conclusion is reached, physical abuse will remain too common.

Neglect

Carla reached into her pocket for the key. Her younger sister and brother waited expectantly for her to open the door. She instinctively put her finger to her lips and cautioned them to be quiet as they entered the apartment. Her mother, she knew, was working, but she didn't know about her mother's boyfriend. Often, he was there, sleeping during the day, which is why they had to be quiet. He became very angry if they were loud coming home from school and woke him up.

But today he wasn't home, so Carla could relax. Her brother and sister went to put their school things away, while she headed into the kitchen. Depending on when Carla's mother got home, dinner could be several hours away and her siblings had already complained about being hungry. Carla could tell her mother hadn't done any shopping. She'd have to figure something out. The refrigerator contained no milk, only a lone squishy apple. The bag of chips she had picked up with hope contained only crumbs. Her mom's boyfriend had probably eaten all of them before he left. She did, however, find a bag of rice to cook.

Carla washed the dirty saucepan from a few nights before and cooked up rice in water. She peeled and chopped up the best parts of the apple and added them to the rice. A little sugar, plus some cinnamon she borrowed from the nice lady down the hall and, in no time, they all sat down to a hot snack. At least they'd have eaten something if their mother didn't make it home to cook dinner.

Understanding childhood abuse certainly includes overt forms of harm done to children. But what about passive acts of neglect? What about Carla and her siblings? Did they have a roof over their heads? Yes. Were they clothed? Yes. Was there food in the house? Yes. Were they neglected? Yes. We hear on the news when neglected children are harmed by accident or fire. But what about the harm children experience from neglect itself? Expecting a ten-year-old, such as Carla, to care for a five-year-old and a seven-year-old is abusive. Adults have the obligation to care for children. Children should never be expected to bear that responsibility. The weight of that burden stresses and strains a child emotionally and physically—effects that last into adulthood.

Neglect can be difficult to define because it involves the lack of something. In my experience, though, I've listened to adults explaining how, as children, they were left alone for hours at a time, not knowing when a parent or caregiver would return. I've heard of children who were locked out of their houses as punishment for minor offenses. Of being passed off from one adult to another, while the parent was absent for days or weeks at a time. I've heard of several children, like Carla, who were given the responsibility of caring for younger siblings, terrified that anything that went wrong would be their fault.

I've heard stories of not enough to eat, not having the right shoes or clothes to wear. Some women have talked, with shame, about having to fend for themselves as young teens for hygiene products. I've heard stories of sheer terror in which children were riding in cars with adults who were drunk or high. I've heard stories of children who were not allowed to go to the doctor or who were refused medicine because the expense was too high or the money simply went toward something else. Neglect, I believe, is the lack of appropriate attention and concern. When neglect happens to children, lives—both physical and emotional—are at risk.

What did you lack growing up? Were you even allowed to be a child or were you thrust into handling adult responsibilities and situations far too early? Were the burdens of adulthood shifted from a parent or other adult onto you? These burdens could have been shifted, not out of malice or hostility, but because of a parent's or caregiver's physical or mental illness. These adults couldn't or wouldn't provide what was needed. Do any of these examples sound like what you dealt with as a child? If so, you grew up settling for less, making do with what little you had, reliant on your creativity, ingenuity, and energy to fend for yourself or take care of others. Aspects of your childhood were stolen from you.

Neglect occurs when an adult disregards the appropriate care a child requires. In some ways, I have come to believe that neglect has the capacity to play an increasing role in the face of childhood abuse. In our fast-paced, do-it-now society, urgency can overtake importance. Adults, pressured from all sides, can make choices that elevate work or other relationships above what is best for children. With so many avenues for adult distraction, I'm fearful that children will continue to be overlooked and, too often, neglected.

Sexual Abuse

One's childhood can be stolen through so many types of abuse, including sexual abuse. Sexual abuse can be defined as exposing children to inappropriate sexuality through what they see, hear, or experience. Childhood sexual abuse can happen through the overt actions of others or the failure to shield children from sexual content or behaviors.

Randy remembers his father always had what he called "girlie" magazines around when he was young. Far from keeping this material away from Randy, his father encouraged Randy to look, telling him that's what he needed to do to be "a man." Randy's father had a way of making the time they spent looking at the magazines together special and grown-up. But some of what Randy saw made him afraid. He didn't understand what the people were doing to one another. Sometimes it looked as though they were hurting one another, but Randy's father made those pictures seem especially important.

By the fifth grade, Randy said he'd seen every sex position possible between men and women, between men and men, and between women and women. He would have trouble, sometimes, looking at a new teacher and wondering if, underneath her clothes, she looked like any of the pictures he had seen. As an adult, he couldn't seem to get that habit out of his head; just like he couldn't seem to get those pictures out of his head or control his need to keep looking at those pictures.

Was Randy sexually molested? No. Was he physically touched in an inappropriate way? No. Was Randy sexually abused? Yes. Randy's father passed his pornography addiction on to his son. As a young child, Randy was exposed to sexual content without any way to put what he was seeing or feeling into a healthy context. Randy was used sexually by his father, who gained gratification in sharing his own sexual addiction. Childhood, and its sexual innocence, was stolen from Randy.

The innocence of childhood was also stolen from Monica, beginning when she was nine. That was the year her mother married Jeff, and Brian came to live with them. Brian was Jeff's thirteen-year-old son. At first, Monica was excited to have an older brother. She thought he was someone who would help and protect her.

Instead, Brian ended up using her. He told her it would be fun; it was a game they could play but had to stay secret. Brian showed her what to do and what he liked. Monica wasn't sure at first, but Brian kept telling her it would be okay, as long as they didn't tell anyone. He gave her candy and took her out for walks. Of course, he had things he wanted to do on those walks, but, sometimes, they'd go for ice cream—after.

Brian would tell her how special and pretty she was, but Monica didn't always feel that way. She did learn what boys liked and what boys expected. In middle school, when the other girls were talking about boys, Monica already knew a lot. Sometimes this made her feel as though she was better than the other girls. But sometimes it didn't.

While my experience is that sexual abuse is the least common of childhood abuse, my fear is that childhood sexual abuse may grow. In the past, childhood sexual abuse was more narrowly defined as physical acts. We've come to an understanding, however, that childhood sexual abuse can involve the emotional and intellectual sexual violation of children as well as the physical.

I have been concerned for years about the societal pattern of the early sexualization of children, especially girls. Children should not be seen as merely nascent adults. Childhood is a precious state of humanity, which needs to be acknowledged as special and protected from undue sexual pressure or influence.

Forcing children into sexual situations and exposing them to sex too early, I fear, is becoming more common. In our fast-paced, hurry-up world, I firmly believe children need to be allowed to develop their sexuality in an age-appropriate, healthy way. To preserve their innocence, children need to be shielded and protected by adults from the increasingly graphic and pervasive sexual content in our culture. To do less is to bring sexual harm to children and the adults they become. Sexualization is a form of childhood abuse and needs to become less common, not more.

Childhood should be a time of joy, discovery, possibilities, and promise. Abuse steals that childhood away. As I said before, children, by nature, should be protected and nurtured by those stronger and more powerful. Yet children who are abused find themselves in targeted, unprotected situations that put them at risk. Pretending the abuse, in whatever form or forms it occurred, wasn't so bad or is just something to get over won't bring about the healing so desperately needed. The damage from abuse establishes a stronghold in a person's life, continuing to create negative effects.

3

The Cost of Survival

Allison felt the urge to flee within her. Life, even at its best, was a constant battle to keep the fears at bay. When she was younger, Allison would take refuge in the back closet, past the folding chairs and winter coats. Close out the world; close out the noise; hide away. She didn't want to hear or see what happened when her parents fought. She'd learned to get out of and stay out of their way. Now, in her twenties, her apartment was the only dark hole she could crawl into, but lately, even that wasn't enough. At some point, she always had to come out.

It was three days before the presentation she was scheduled to give at work and her panic was becoming unbearable. Allison didn't want to tell her supervisor no, but how was she going to stand up in front of people, exposed like that? They'd stare at her and judge her and hate what she had to say. Allison asked herself why she'd ever agreed to do such a dangerous thing in the first place. Of course, she knew the answer: she'd been too afraid to say no. Afraid to say yes and afraid to say no—just afraid, with nowhere to hide. Sometimes life outside the closet just didn't seem worth it.

Abused children can become extremely adept at finding ways to survive within abusive situations. These survival strategies are borne out of desperation. They are crafted from a child's incomplete understanding of what is happening and why. These strategies achieve a level of effectiveness and the abused child learns to rely on them. However, over time, these strategies can complicate and damage the path to functional maturity. Stopgap, short-term, in-the-moment, whatever-it-takes strategies are ill-suited to long-term propositions, such as adulthood, maturity, and especially, relationships.

Over the years, I've come to recognize how childhood abuse survival strategies metastasize into adult maladaptive patterns. I don't use the term *maladaptive* lightly. Maladaptive means incomplete, inadequate, or faulty adaptation. I also do not use maladaptive pejoratively. I am constantly amazed by the ways children find to adapt to the horrible. Such is the resiliency of children.

This childhood resiliency, however, can harden over time into adult resistance. In some ways, these protective strategies come to define a person's identity. These protective measures that became woven into the fabric of childhood become a mess of complicated threads to untangle as adults.

Trust Factor

Jason learned growing up that those close to you could get past your protective guard and hurt you. The safest thing to do was to keep people out. But Jason also knew that to get ahead in life, people expected you to be personable and friendly. You needed to, at least, give the appearance of being open; you needed, for example, to be able to make and take jokes. Jason hated jokes; they weren't funny and people only told them as a way to put you down. But he learned to keep that reaction hidden, to force himself to smile and laugh. Jason wore a mask of friendliness on the outside and kept his distrust and suspicion on the inside. As a result, he was acquainted with many but friends with few. Jason realized early on that the only person he could really trust was himself.

Gina learned early on not to trust herself. Making decisions on her own was stressful, while asking others was much easier. People would always be available to tell her what to do and how to do it. Gina knew that if she tried to do things her way, she'd fail. If she did what others said, then she could at least attempt to deflect some of the blame when things didn't go well. And people didn't yell at her for wanting to do something different. Gina knew people wouldn't like her for who she was. She learned to find out what they liked and then try her hardest to become just that. Empty inside, Gina relied on others to fill her up.

Children who are abused may adapt by distorting who and when to trust. Childhood abuse warps a child's understanding of and ability to trust. Children, who are incredibly vulnerable, must trust the adults who care for them. When those adults are untrustworthy, children can draw different conclusions. Like Jason, some children conclude that trust is a precious commodity to be hoarded. These children tend to isolate and draw on their own resources to function. Others, like Gina, learn to distrust themselves and rely solely on others. Children like Jason are closed doors who let in no one. Children like Gina are wide-open doors who let in everyone.

Life on High Alert

Cindy glanced at the clock, feeling her breathing increase. He was late. Maybe he wouldn't come tonight. She could always hope. Then again, maybe it was just better to get it over with, at least for a while. Waiting, in some ways, was worse. At least when it was happening, she knew it would soon be over. Waiting meant it hadn't begun. Oddly, the only time Cindy was safe from him was right after it happened. She could always count on a lull; just as she could always count on the lull ending.

Stephen really wanted to go to the game. Why wasn't anything easy? All his friends were going and had been laughing and talking about what a fun time they'd have. The game was a big deal; he had to be there. But, first, he had to get his mom to agree. As he rounded the corner in his neighborhood, Stephen went over in his mind every reason she could give not to let him go. He needed to find a way around each of her objections. Of course, Stephen told himself he had to be careful. He couldn't give the impression he was arguing; that always set her off. Presentation and timing were everything. Mention the game when she was distracted by something else and make going seem like no big deal. If she knew how much the game meant to him, she might say yes, but she'd also find a way to make him pay.

Children who are abused may adapt by retaining a habit of constant vigilance—as though they're constantly under a state of siege. Their worlds are populated not by security but by patterns of risk and attack. On a regular basis, or on a whim, they know they can become the targets of harm. Watching out for such harm, planning for it, attempting to forestall it, and finding ways to survive it create a life lived on high alert. Paradoxically, such children can experience more stress when harm is not occurring. The storm becomes the known; calm is unknown and, therefore, suspect.

Playing the Blame Game

Allan knew what his father was going to say when he saw the test results. He would yell and tell him he wasn't trying hard enough. He would name off all the men in the family and what they had accomplished. He'd talk about his own schooling and how much different his results were from Allan's. He'd ask why Allan didn't try harder; as if trying harder was the answer to everything. Allan did try hard; he tried so hard he made himself sick. Even thinking about taking that test, or any test, made him sick. Sick, because Allan was afraid his father was right. He wasn't good enough. No matter how hard Allan tried, he could never be or do enough. He didn't deserve to be in his family.

Mindy didn't deserve to be in her family either. She knew that. She wasn't as cute as her sister. She wasn't as popular as her brother. Mindy wasn't like the rest of the family. When they would go out together, her parents would talk to the other two. The only time they acknowledged Mindy was to tell her to hurry up when she lagged too far behind. That was always confusing; why did they want her along when they treated her like she didn't belong? Maybe they just liked to yell at her. Mindy, get over here! Mindy, go over there! Mindy, why can't you do this? Mindy, why did you do that? She didn't have two people telling her what to do, she had four. All of them were somehow angry she wasn't who they wanted her to be. Her family didn't like her and it was all her fault.

Children who are abused may adapt by accepting blame for the abuse. One primary reason for accepting responsibility is that abusers so often tell children they are to blame. They are told they are to blame because they aren't good enough or smart enough—or, conversely, because they think they are too good or act as if they're so smart. They are blamed for being too ugly or, conversely, for being too pretty and, thus, causing the abuse. Their actions or inactions are used as a reason for the abuse. Such children are in a no-win situation.

I believe another primary reason children accept blame for their abuse is to attempt to have some measure of control over the situation. If I am doing something to cause my abuse, then maybe I can find a way to change and stop the abuse. If I'm not to blame, I have no control; if I am to blame, then maybe I have some control.

Assuming the Worst

Ellen didn't think twice when her friend asked her to try out for the play. The answer, of course, was no. Even though Ellen badly wanted to be in the play, there was just no way. She wouldn't be chosen. She'd stand up there and audition and be told, in front of all those people, "We don't want you." Why would she do that to herself? She already knew the outcome; she had no reason to try. So, when her friend asked, Ellen told her she'd already signed up for the stage crew, which Ellen planned to do right after third period. Stage crew accepted anybody. She could still be part of the play—just in the background, where she belonged.

As soon as Tim entered the room, he noticed Tiffany look away. He knew it. He knew she didn't like him, no matter what his friends were trying to tell him. They'd convinced him to go to the party, against his better judgment, saying Tiffany would be there and she liked him. No, she didn't. He no more walked into the room and she couldn't stand to look at him; she turned away. That made Tim mad. He hadn't asked her to like him. He didn't care if she liked him or not. She was similar to all the other girls who didn't want to have anything to do with him. Forget her. Forget what his friends told him. Forget the party. He'd have more fun at home playing video games.

Children who are abused may adapt by assuming the worst. Instead of hoping for something good, they protect themselves by assuming something bad. In this way, they are not surprised when things go wrong. If I expect good things and they don't happen, then I'm disappointed. If I expect bad things and they happen, then at least I'm right.

Aches and Pains

Brad didn't feel well. His stomach and head hurt, his fingers felt tingly, and his heart was beating hard. He kept telling his mother he didn't want to go to school, but she wouldn't listen. She kept saying she was going to be late for work and he had better get himself up and dressed or she would take him to school in his pajamas. What if she really did? What if the kids at school made fun of him? He would have to go, even though he felt sick. His mother didn't like it when he was sick. She would roll her eyes and raise her voice and tell him all the things she had to change because he was sick. Whenever Brad was sick, telling his mother made him feel worse because she always seemed to get angry.

Tamara could feel her back tighten. She shifted, as much as she could, trying to get comfortable in the back seat. She might try to climb into the front and put down the seat, but she was afraid to risk it. Tamara's father told her she had to stay in the back seat because he didn't want anyone to see she was in the car. That had happened once; the police got called and Tamara was told it was her fault. From then on, she had to lie down in the back seat and not get up so no one could see her. Her father said he didn't want to get in trouble again for Tamara being in the car so long. If he got in trouble, it would be her fault because she didn't do what she was supposed to. So Tamara squirmed and shifted and tried to find a position that was comfortable after so long. The weird thing was, lately, after she got out of the car, her back still hurt.

Children who are abused may adapt by substituting a physical hurt for an emotional hurt. When asked if something is wrong, they will respond with a physical ailment, which might be real or could be psychosomatic. Unable to comprehend their emotional hurt, they latch on to a physical complaint as the reason for their discomfort. The physical pain becomes the focus for their emotional pain. These children are highly susceptible to self-harm as they grow older, using physical pain as a release point for emotional distress.

Waving the White Flag

Jessica was sad. She really liked Amber, but now Hannah and Amber were friends. Hannah told Amber she couldn't be friends with Jessica. Jessica didn't want to fight with Amber, and she really didn't want to fight with Hannah. Hannah was mean; she'd even gotten in trouble for hitting another girl at recess. Jessica didn't want Hannah to hit her next. So, even though she was sad, Jessica knew the best thing to do was to avoid Amber. She already avoided Hannah. Alexis told Jessica she should stand up to Amber and Hannah, but that never worked. Sticking up for yourself meant making other people mad at you; Jessica knew that. Mad people had to be avoided because they were unsafe. Mad people said and did things that hurt others, and they never seemed to feel sorry about doing so. Jessica knew the best thing to do was get away from mad people, even if it meant giving up things she wanted.

Trent didn't know what to tell Mr. Woodson. He was going to be so disappointed and ask Trent why he hadn't completed the application for the music camp. He would remind Trent how he had gone to bat for him and written to the director in order to even get Trent an application. He'd want to know why he had gone to all that trouble if Trent was going to blow off doing anything about applying. Trent would do his best to thank him for the effort. He'd try to explain that he couldn't go because his dad had already signed him up for a football camp the same month. If Trent didn't go to the football camp, he'd never hear the end of it at home all summer. The choice between disappointing Mr. Woodson and disappointing his dad wasn't even close. Mr. Woodson would be disappointed; his dad would make his life miserable.

Children who are abused may adapt by giving in to the demands of others without overt objection. Instead, they stuff and internalize their disappointment, anger, and frustration. Life becomes a predictable series of losses to be tolerated.

Good Little Soldier or Little Miss Perfect

Charlie worshiped his grandfather. When Papaw said to jump, Charlie asked how high. He wanted to be just like Papaw. Papaw wanted Charlie to be just like him too. Papaw did not want Charlie turning out like his father, whom Papaw did not approve of. Papaw was very alert to ways Charlie was becoming like his father and would discipline Charlie for his own good. Charlie was terrified of disappointing Papaw and being like his father, even though he didn't remember anything about his father because he was very young when he left. Now, the only things Charlie knew about his father were negative.

Miranda checked herself in the mirror before leaving her bedroom. She twisted this way and that, looking from all angles. Her jeans needed to be tight but not too tight. Her top needed to be snug but not too snug. Her makeup needed to reach that difficult balance of visible but not apparent. Miranda grabbed her backpack and exited her room, knowing a second inspection was coming before she could get out the front door for school. What was she wearing? How did it look? Had she done her homework? Was that work not only correct but neat and legible? She had to always adhere to certain standards. Her family wasn't like other families. Miranda had a reputation to uphold, a reputation of more than competence—but one of excellence. Most days, Miranda felt up to the challenge. On the days she didn't, Miranda fretted and worried and dreamt of disaster. All she had to do was be the best, every day, all the time, no matter what.

Children who are abused may adapt by attempting to perfectly fulfill the expectations of others. These children become highly adept at interpreting the desires of others, while the ability to understand their own desires atrophies. In addition, perfection becomes the impossible standard they reach for, their ledge of safety, always visible but rarely attained and, even then, not for long.

Finding Comfort

Shelby couldn't tear open the package quick enough. She had only a short time to devour her treat before someone came home. Her sister would be nosey and might tell on her for eating something she wasn't supposed to. If Shelby's mother came home and caught her, Shelby would be scolded for eating "junk" and would have her dinner taken away. But the treat was just so delicious. So much in Shelby's life was hard to swallow, but not this. She was sure she could eat a mountain of these treats and never feel full. Creamy and sweet, they melted in her mouth. For one blissful moment, Shelby was at peace.

Evan took a deep drag, filling his lungs as far as they would go. When he had done that in the past, he had coughed his lungs out, but not anymore. Amazing how you get used to things. Cigarettes helped him feel energized, took the edge off his hunger, and provided a shield to keep others away. Too young to buy them at the store, Evan was usually able to pocket three or four when his dad was passed out. His dad would never remember whether he smoked them, as long as Evan made sure to get most of the smell off himself before he went home. Other kids his age smoked to feel or look cool. He smoked to feel good. For one blissful moment, Evan was at peace.

Children who are abused may adapt by looking to outside sources for relief and comfort. If people are unreliable and unpredictable, children who are abused may find certain behaviors and substances appealing because they appear more constant and certain. Children turn to a variety of outside sources to feel better: food, cigarettes, drugs, alcohol, sexual activity, video games—just about anything that produces a pleasure or reward response. When life is one disappointment after another, why not find whatever pleasure you can?

Survival Strategies

Clearly, people who were abused as children can be highly adaptive, finding creative ways to survive the abuse. All these survival strate gies, of course, come with a cost. What works in the moment to numb or alleviate the pain can cause collateral damage in the long term. These costs can be extensive and can complicate a person's emotional, intellectual, physical, relational, and spiritual health. These costs eventually become unavoidable, no matter how fast or far you try to outrun them.

4

The Violation
of Emotional Abuse

Craig's mother was never around much. He remembered knowing she'd been at the house because a gallon of milk would appear in the refrigerator. There was usually food in the house, but sometimes, it just wasn't what Craig wanted. As Craig hit high school, his part-time job washing dishes at a local restaurant meant not just money but whatever leftovers Craig could snatch off dirty plates. He had little reason to go home; his mother never seemed to, though Craig wasn't exactly sure where she spent most of her time. He told himself to stop caring so much about her because she didn't seem to care much about him.

Brittany's mother was always around. She never seemed to leave the house, at least when Brittany was there. She wanted to know where Brittany was, what she was doing, who she was talking to. There was always food in the house, but it was tightly controlled by her mother, who didn't like anything artificial or processed. Brittany remembered trading whatever she could for the cookies in other kids' lunchboxes, especially Oreos. Brittany wished her mother would get a life and stop telling her how to live hers.

Dustin's father was nothing if not predictable. He rarely said two words to Dustin unless Dustin did something wrong, and then it might be four. Correct performance, as defined by his father, was a given in their household—nothing to be commented on and certainly nothing to be complimented. No was the automatic response to most requests, accompanied by a tone and manner that indicated Dustin was foolish to even ask. His father was like a rock in the middle of the river—immovable, requiring Dustin to maneuver around him to get where he wanted to go.

The only predictable thing about Emily's dad was his unpredictability. His moods and opinions were all over the map. Emily was never quite sure what triggered him to react a certain way yesterday and a completely different way today. She never knew which father she had to deal with. Was he the kind, funny Good Dad or the moody, sarcastic Bad Dad? Because she was able to read his moods, she learned when to be invisible and when it seemed safe to come out.

Four different people. Four different experiences, sometimes completely opposite. Or are they? Can opposite actions cause equivalent damage? As always, the question seems to be, when does a person cross over a line from merely acting badly to being emotionally abusive? How can you possibly define what it looks like when emotional abuse in childhood can take so many forms?

As I've already stated, we tend to deny the truth of our own childhood abuse. We may react when we observe abusive behavior in the grocery store aisle between a parent and child but doggedly refuse to see it within the content of our memories. The challenge, then, is twofold—to understand the general signs of childhood emotional abuse and, once understood, to use that lens to view our childhood experiences.

Understanding Childhood Emotional Abuse

Can a concept, such as childhood emotional abuse, with so many layers, be culled down into some sort of a checklist? Can determining an emotionally abusive childhood be as simple as "yes" if you check box A but "no" if you check box B? In my experience, childhood emotional abuse doesn't work that way. However, while the experiences of childhood emotional abuse are highly personal, some boxes can always be checked. Patterns and types of behaviors have been identified as psychologically and emotionally damaging to children and the adults they grow into. These behaviors can be understood as abusive when they are present with consistency and/or severity.

However, some may counter, "This or that happened only once or twice." Is that still abusive? The keys to understanding the concept of emotional abuse are both consistency and severity. Yes, childhood emotional abuse occurs within an ongoing pattern of emotionally damaging behaviors, but it can also occur within a single, emotionally traumatizing event. Whether the emotional abuse is a consistent set of behaviors or a single, damaging event, it is considered abuse because an adult has clearly demonstrated a disregard for a child's welfare.

For those of you who are still conflicted over events in your past, I offer the following behaviors that I have found to be emotionally damaging and, therefore, abusive. They come from what I have read and studied, what I have experienced in my life, and what I have heard from the lives of others. They aren't meant to represent an all-inclusive list but, rather, to point the way to a type of behavior that robs children of love, attention, affirmation, affection, security, safety, and care. Some of these examples you'll agree with and some you won't. If you come to an example and think to yourself, *That can't be abuse*, I ask you to pay special attention. The example may have triggered an "it wasn't so bad" defense mechanism.

Unrealistic Expectations

Caleb was getting really worried. He squirmed in his seat and gathered up the courage to explain to his father, again, that he really, really needed to go to the bathroom. Caleb understood he should have gone when they stopped for gas. But, truly, he hadn't needed to then. He more than did now. His tummy hurt, and his head throbbed listening to his parents argue about stopping the car. Caleb was scared when they argued about him. If they kept arguing but didn't stop, he was scared he'd wet his pants.

"I have to go now!" Caleb finally screamed over the raised voices of his parents. His father said a word he wasn't supposed to and veered the car over to the side of the road. Caleb could tell his father was mad as he came around to the door, pulled it open, and lifted Caleb out by the arm. Without stopping to let Caleb unzip his pants, his father just yanked them down around his knees, right there on the side of the road and ordered him to pee while he watched. Embarrassed and confused, Caleb couldn't, at first, which seemed to make his father even angrier. His father yelled, "This is why you don't take a five-year-old on a car trip!"

Emotional abuse happens when an adult places unrealistic expectations on a child and then punishes the child, through words and actions, for failure to perform.

Most children are compliant and try to do what adults ask them to do. Children have a desire to meet the expectations placed on them; they want to gain the approval of those they look up to, love, and respect. When unrealistic expectations are placed on a child, no amount of desire on the child's part can overcome such a high bar. Children then see themselves as failures; they internalize the blame for not meeting the expectations. Children, especially young children, do not have the capacity to understand they are in a no-win situation.

These unrealistic expectations could be set in regard to something physical, such as the ability to control one's bladder, being expected to carry heavy items or a large number of objects without dropping any, or walking a long distance at an adult pace. Each of these creates the expectation that the child must react physically as an adult while still being a child.

Unrealistic expectations can also involve something intellectual, such as performing at a certain level in school or understanding how to react in certain situations or knowing the answer to a difficult question. Unrealistic expectations can also center on something emotional, such as being expected to react to a challenging situation with uncharacteristic maturity or patience. When these unrealistic expectations are presented, all the child knows is they aren't good enough or strong enough or patient enough or smart enough to succeed. When such expectations are put on a child at a time of high stress or high stakes, the message that they are a failure can be indelibly written on their heart and mind. When such unrealistic expectations are routine, the weight of a "you-are-not-enough" message can suppress a child's natural emotional buoyancy

Showing Hostility

"Just hurry up, will you?" Alicia heard her mother yell out the window. She attempted to walk-run to the car, even though Alicia knew she wasn't supposed to run on the school sidewalk. "I don't know why you're always so late," her mother muttered as Alicia got into the car. Sighing deeply, her mother eyed the rearview mirror and pulled away from the curb, declaring, "You should have been here ten minutes ago." Alicia could feel the familiar tension in her stomach. Her mother was in one of those moods in which she was mad at everything and Alicia couldn't do anything right. Alicia thought about explaining that Mr. Hernandez had kept her a few minutes after class to talk about her collage, which he wanted to put up in the glass case by the office. She had been so proud to tell her mother, but now she knew she'd better wait.

Emotional abuse happens when an adult uses a child as a convenient receptacle for hostility and negativity that have nothing to do with the child.

Those who are perceived as weaker, for whatever reason, can become convenient targets for the hostility of others. Animals are a known target, as evidenced by the work of organizations such as the SPCA (Society for the Prevention of Cruelty to Animals). Children, sadly, also fall within that hierarchy of power and control. They can become punching bags on which adults vent their anger, frustration, irritation, annoyance, or any emotional negativity. Often this negativity vented on children is in no way directly connected to them. Children become, as they say, collateral damage to an adult at war with the world.

Adults who take out their anger on children rarely are truthful about the source of that anger and hostility. Some shift the blame unfairly to their punching bag of choice, placing the burden of their actions, as well as the reasons for the actions, on the child. Others leave the reasons for the negativity unexplained. In either case, the child is left to conclude they are responsible, through either direct indictment or indirect inference.

Threatening

"Don't make me come up there!" Elliott should have been in bed more than thirty minutes ago, but he'd gotten caught up in the video game he was playing. If he'd been quieter, his father wouldn't have known he was still awake. Elliott played this game every night—oh, not the video game, the game with his dad. At least once a night, Elliott would hear "Don't make me come up there!" bellowed from downstairs. The game was to figure out how quickly his dad would get mad and yell at him. Tonight, Elliott knew he'd been too loud, but some nights his father could yell about anything. If his father was mad enough to come up, Elliott would be in a lot of trouble, with no telling what privileges he would take away. Elliott was told repeatedly that nothing he had was his. "I put food on the table, clothes on your back, and a roof over your head," his father never forgot to remind him. The implied threat was, at any time, an essential item could be snatched away for bad behavior. The secret was not to show you cared too much about anything. That's why Elliott made sure to play with the dog when his father wasn't around.

Emotional abuse happens when an adult threatens consequences that rarely happen but when they do are inappropriately severe.

Children need structure and stability to get their balance in the world. Within an atmosphere of constant threats, children lose a sense of security. They begin to doubt and distrust. When nothing is safe, they hoard and become secretive to protect what is most vital to them.

If threats are verbalized but never materialize, children can falsely conclude they are immune from negative consequences. They may feel disdain toward and disrespect for authority figures. They may become unpleasantly surprised when consequences actually happen.

Competing

Both Tina and Shelly knew their mother was itching for a fight. They recognized the signs. The two girls had been talking about something they saw on television when, suddenly, their mother was butting into their conversation. Normally, she paid little attention to their adolescent banter—but not today. She was upset about something and was looking for a place to vent. Tina, as usual, found a way to vacate the vicinity; she never stayed around to finish a fight. Shelly, however, always did, staying engaged with their angry or frustrated mother for as long as it took, arguing her points right back, and even risking punishments for being "mouthy" and "disrespectful." Tina never stayed in the ring; Shelly stayed until the final bell. Neither girl "won." The outcome of these unfair fights was an adult and two teenagers who were disgruntled, unsatisfied, and angry at one another. Tina and Shelly's mother was mad at them both; Tina was mad at her mother for picking the fight and at Shelly for "making it worse"; and Shelly was mad at her mother for continuing to engage her and at Tina for being a "coward." After one of these verbal battles, the three of them wouldn't talk to one another for days.

Emotional abuse happens when an adult engages in unfair competition with a child because the adult desires to win and elevate themselves on the back of the child.

Healthy competition is a great way for people to test their capabilities; children need to be stretched and tested and shown how much they are able to accomplish. This unhealthy competition, however, is a rigged game. I've seen this happen verbally between adults and children, as in the case of Tina and Shelly. I've seen this happen athletically, with an adult challenging a child to a physical contest the child has no chance of winning. I've seen this happen intellectually, with an adult intentionally speaking beyond a child's capacity to understand, while egging the child on to try anyway.

Blaming

"I can't believe I've got to do this all over again," Ruby's mother said wearily, as she began to unpack Ruby's school backpack.

"Why do they send home all of these stupid papers?" Ruby knew her mother was unhappy but couldn't decide about what. "Make sure your parents see these papers," she was told. Ruby did and now her mother was unhappy.

Standing quietly, she watched as her mother talked to herself, sorting the papers into piles. Her mother was so absorbed, Ruby wasn't sure she even realized Ruby was there. "Just had to have another baby," her mother muttered. "Couldn't stop at three; no, just had to have another." Ruby had heard her mother say this before. One of her brothers was already out of the house, the other in high school, and her sister was in middle school. Ruby didn't know why it took so long for her parents to have her, but she'd overheard the word *mistake* when they talked about her. Other people laughed, but Ruby didn't think it was funny to be a mistake. Ruby was sure her mother would be happier if Ruby hadn't been born, so she tried hard to do everything right so her mother would change her mind. Too often, though, Ruby didn't understand what the right thing was. She thought the right thing was to bring home the papers, but doing so made her mother unhappy.

Emotional abuse happens when an adult blames a child for circumstances outside of the child's control or responsibility.

Children can become receptacles of blame, convenient repositories where adults place the consequences of their own actions. Without knowing any different, when children are told "you're the reason," they believe it. This type of abuse is especially damaging when, as in Ruby's case, the dissatisfaction is not so much with what the child does but with who the child is.

Humiliating

"My God! You are so clumsy! What is wrong with you?" Once again, Angie had spilled her milk. Her siblings popped up out of their seats, as much to get away from their mother as away from the milk, which was now spreading across the table and threatening to drip on the floor.

"Get out of my way!" their mother yelled as she grabbed a kitchen towel and headed for the spill. "Don't just stand there! Pick up those plates so I can make sure it doesn't get on the carpet!"

Angie was afraid to move, afraid to do anything else wrong. No one looked at her—not her mother, not her brother, not her sister—until the spill was mopped up and the table put back together.

"Oh, no you don't," her mother said as Angie started to sit down at the table. "You cannot be trusted." After picking up Angie's plate, her mother went into the kitchen and placed it on the floor, next to the dog bowl. "You can just eat with the dog until you can eat like a person." With that, her mother marched back into the other room, leaving Angie thinking about a meal she no longer had any interest in.

Emotional abuse happens when an adult humiliates a child for actions consistent with being a child.

Children require correction from adults to learn the right thing to do. Emotional abuse happens when correction meant to help the child is turned into humiliation meant to punish the child. The definition of humiliation is to cause a painful loss of dignity, pride, or self-respect. Children have not yet gained the maturity to withstand the damage of humiliation, which can be difficult even for adults to endure. Humiliating a child is taking advantage of someone younger and more vulnerable out of a distorted desire for control and power.

Minimizing

Jimmy heard the crack of the bat and watched as the ball soared up in an arch from the T-ball stand. Feeling both terrified and thrilled, he realized the ball was headed right to him. He had to catch this ball—that was his job as an outfielder. The mitt felt like it weighed a hundred pounds as he tried to maneuver it into place, all the while watching the ball. Pop! The ball barely missed his mitt and glanced off his left cheek. Startled, Jimmy reacted instantly, letting out a yelp. Tears sprang to his eyes.

"Are you okay?" Carlos asked, running over to him. Jimmy was crying so hard at that point, he couldn't answer, the ball lying forgotten a few feet away.

"James!" he heard his father call out, as he came out onto the field. "Let me look at you." Blinking furiously, Jimmy tried to stop crying.

"You're fine," his father concluded. "Don't be a baby. You just got hit by a ball. Next time, catch it and that won't happen." His father turned and walked off the field.

"Are you okay?" Carlos asked again. Jimmy wasn't sure. His father said he was fine, but Jimmy didn't feel that way.

Emotional abuse happens when an adult minimizes or invalidates a child's appropriate reaction.

Emotional abuse happens when an adult minimizes a child's thoughts and feelings as inaccurate or unreliable. The child reacts appropriately to what they are feeling but is told by the adult that those reactions are faulty. The child learns to distrust those feelings and to see themselves as faulty as well. Some adults may choose to minimize a child's feelings out of discomfort at experiencing those feelings secondhand. But when adults marginalize the feelings of children, they marginalize the child.

Favoring

"Stop that, please!" Maria's mother blurted out. Maria hadn't realized she was fingering the clothes on the rack. She was just

61

bored. They'd been out shopping for what seemed like hours and Maria wanted to go home or at least find a place to sit down.

"Your sister never acted this way," her mother muttered, scooting hanger after hanger around the display. Maria had no idea what her mother was looking for and was afraid her mother didn't either. Her mother didn't seem to like anything she saw today, including Maria. Of course, Maria understood she was at fault because she wasn't like her big sister, Susanna. Susanna and her mother were best friends. Her mother never seemed to yell at Susanna, who did everything correctly. Susanna was tall and thin and accomplished at school; Maria wasn't any of those things. With Susanna getting ready to go off to college, Maria had secretly hoped things would get better with her mother. Now, she wasn't so sure. Her mother would probably still go on loving Susanna more, even when Susanna was gone.

Emotional abuse happens when an adult shows an obvious preference for one child in the family over another.

Preferring one child over another is as old as the Bible. This does not, however, make favoring one child over another right. Children need the love and affection of parents. When a parent withholds love and affection, the relationship with the child is harmed. When a parent withholds love and affection from one child and then lavishes it on another child, the relationship between the parent and the other child is harmed, as well as the relationship between the two children. The family becomes a battleground, with family members pitted against other family members for supremacy.

Acting Indifferent

"Are you going to the party on Saturday?" Will asked Kevin, keeping his voice down and darting his eyes up and down the hallway. You never knew who might be listening, and the party wasn't really for middle school kids. No parents and lots of high schoolers.

"Of course," Kevin answered.

"What are you going to tell your parents?" Will still hadn't figured that out himself and was hoping Kevin might have a helpful suggestion.

"I'm not going to tell them anything," Kevin said. "They don't care what I do."

Will looked impressed. "Wow!"

"It's not a big deal," Kevin explained. "My mom will be working, so she won't even know, and my dad couldn't care less."

"Wow," Will said again. "My parents always want to know what I'm doing."

"Not mine. They let me do what I want." Kevin shrugged, picking up his backpack.

"I wish my parents were like yours," Will admitted.

No, you don't, Kevin thought to himself.

Emotional abuse happens when an adult who should be watching out for a child's best interests chooses not to.

Children are not the best judges of what is good or bad, safe or hazardous. For this reason, adults are given charge over them. Within a family situation, this authority over children is best combined with love and affection. Saying yes and saying no are accompanied by an explanation of why, which teaches the child to trust the adult and gain valuable lessons for the future. These opportunities are squandered when a parent or adult refuses, for whatever reason, to positively monitor a child's actions and activities. Children left to their own devices are often at significant risk. They are at risk in the moment and at risk in the future. In the moment, they are at risk because they are unable to judge the best course. In the future, they are at risk because they weren't taught how to judge the best course for the next time.

Infantilizing

"Let me do that for you!" Before Janae had time to protest, her mother was reaching across the table, grabbing up the plate the waiter had just delivered. "You know what happens when you take too big of bites." Janae's mother swiftly diced the piece of chicken. "Oh, this is far too many fries. You don't need that much," her mom said, taking half of what Janae was looking forward to eating and sweeping it onto her own plate. The waiter had already been told Janae was too young for pop and could only have milk.

Before stopping at the restaurant, they'd gone shopping for school clothes. She had avoided the little kids' department only because she'd outgrown the biggest size there. "I don't want you to grow up!" her mother had wailed loudly at that realization. "You're my baby girl forever!" And she'd gathered her up and hugged her hard, right in the middle of the store. The way Janae's mother treated her was frustrating. But she couldn't cry; that would just make it worse.

Emotional abuse happens when an adult treats a child in a way that denies their age or experience.

Children are not meant to be children forever. Their natural progression is to grow, mature, and create an adult life and mature relationships. When children are kept artificially trapped in childhood, they can become stunted, insecure adults. Some adults, for their own reasons, may seek to keep a child in an artificial, immature state. When this happens, the adult places their needs above the needs of the child.

Isolating

The answer was no, Derek knew that, so he didn't even ask. He'd told Jackson he couldn't go and gave some excuse about going to his uncle's house instead. The truth was, Derek never went to his uncle's house, even though he lived a few miles away. Derek never went anywhere, except to school. He didn't go to friends' houses or have anyone over to his house. This worried Derek because he was afraid he would lose the few friends he had. They couldn't understand why he was never allowed to do anything or go anywhere. No playdates. No parties. No sleepovers.

Instead, when Derek went home, he usually was told to go to his room. Sometimes he was sent to his room as punishment for being too loud or not doing chores or, sometimes, for nothing at all. Derek spent a lot of time in his room. The school year was bad, but summer was really tough. He could hear the kids in the neighborhood playing. Crouching down so he wouldn't be seen, he'd watch them riding their bikes or playing in the neighbors' yards. Sometimes Derek felt he was invisible; at least, no one else in the world seemed to know or care where he was. "I'm here," he'd say to himself as he watched the other kids play. Lately he was starting to doubt even that.

Emotional abuse happens when an adult denies a child access to healthy social interactions with peers, family members, and adults.

Some adults are so absorbed with their own needs, desires, or requirements that they find they have no room in their lives to attend to the same things for the children under their care. They say no not because it's wrong but because of the effort it takes to say yes. The child learns where they rate on that adult's list, which is at the bottom. Isolated and starved for affection and connection, the child is left alone with nowhere to turn.

Withholding Affection

"You don't deserve a hug," Lily's father told her, removing her arms from around his waist. "You haven't done what I asked you to do." When Lily's father walked in the door, she'd been so happy to see him. Now, she was very unhappy.

"What didn't I do?" she asked, confused and upset.

"You know you're supposed to put your bike away in the garage when you're finished riding it. Where is it now?" he asked sternly.

Lily tried to think. She'd been riding her bike, but then Andy had come over to play. What had she done with her bike?

When she didn't answer, her father said, "It's lying in the middle of the front lawn. Go put it away."

Dejected, Lily went outside and did what she was told. There would be no hug today, maybe not even tomorrow. Lily had been bad, although she hadn't meant to be. She just forgot. But her father told her she didn't deserve hugs when she was bad and Lily believed him.

Emotional abuse happens when an adult withholds affection from a child as punishment.

Children should not have to earn affection. Affection should not be a prize that a child must win by adhering to adult rules. Children are lovable and worthy of affection by their very nature. When affection is withheld, not for disobedience but for merely being, a child has no security of receiving that affection. Their childish nature stands as a barrier to ever achieving the desired goal.

Yelling

"Will you kids please just shut up?!" Robbie and Karen looked at each other, wide-eyed. They hadn't thought they were that loud but Stephanie certainly did. Their father had told them that Stephanie wasn't used to kids. It was hard to tell, though, if they'd really been loud or if Stephanie was just mad. She yelled a lot—through a closed door, down the hallway, up the stairs. Robbie thought it was weird that Stephanie never seemed to be with them when she wanted to say something to them. She always yelled. Karen didn't like it; she'd tear up and Robbie would go to her and tell her everything was okay. He would protect her. After Stephanie finished yelling, Karen and Robbie would start playing again, but they would be very, very quiet. They would pretend they were hiding from a terrible monster that would hurt them if they were found.

Emotional abuse happens when an adult routinely uses harsh words and a raised voice to frighten children into compliance.

Yelling or screaming at someone is a violent act, involving anger and fear. Yelling or shouting is meant to signal danger and effect movement. But when a child is yelled at for being a child, where is the danger? The danger comes from the person doing the yelling. The child then generally attempts to move away from the person doing the yelling because they feel insecure, unsafe, and distrustful.

Swearing

"What the (blank) do you think you're doing? Do you have any idea how (blank) much that cost?" Carlee froze, leaving the drawer to the tool rack open. Frank had entered the garage and started yelling. Carlee knew he was really mad because he was using bad words.

"I wasn't going to touch anything," Carlee started to say, to explain why she was in his tools. Frank interrupted her, using more bad words and more yelling, telling her she wasn't supposed to ever get into his stuff.

Carlee stepped away from the tool rack and started to tear up, but that just seemed to make Frank angrier. He yelled at her to stop crying. As soon as Frank said that, Carlee started crying in earnest. She couldn't say that she had gone into Frank's tool rack to see if that's where Bobby had hidden the toy ring she had gotten from the machine at the store. Bobby thought it was funny to hide things from Carlee, especially in places she wasn't supposed to go. All she was trying to do was find what was hers, but now she'd gotten Frank mad enough to use bad words. She was angry at him, angry at Bobby, and angry at herself for not being more careful about where and when to look. Carlee was so mad that she almost said a bad word.

Emotional abuse happens when an adult routinely uses obscene or profane language to communicate with a child.

Swearing, as a form of verbal aggression, can be a substitute for physical aggression. Children understand the aggression behind the use of profane language, if not always the meaning of those words. At home, at school, and at church, children are taught and warned not to use such words. When adults use those words toward them or to describe them, children can become confused and frightened. When adults act in ways children are told is wrong, the rules that keep their world secure appear not to apply. When rules don't apply, children feel unsafe.

Insulting

"You are not going to turn that in," Zach's mother told him matter-of-factly.

"Why not?" he asked, puzzled.

"This is clearly not your best work," his mother informed him, flipping his picture onto the table. "You said you were supposed to be drawing our house. This is not our house."

"Yes, it is," Zach protested, and he started to explain what each part of the picture was. His mother, however, would hear none of it. All she wanted to point out was how poorly he'd drawn, how nothing in the picture made any sense; things weren't the right shape or the right color. "This looks like you spent five minutes slapping something together so you could play your video games," she pronounced.

Zach stopped talking. He didn't explain how long he'd worked on the drawing or how much he liked how his house had turned out.

"Do it over," his mother ordered. "This looks like a five-year-old did it."

Emotional abuse happens when an adult belittles or hypercriticizes a child or a child's efforts.

Children need to be encouraged to do their best work. But insults are not positive encouragement; insults are negative disparagements. Children, like any of us, however, are simply not going to do their "best" all of the time. Expecting a child to hit a home run every time at bat is unrealistic; such an expectation places too heavy a burden on the child. And who is to say what is "best"? A child may have different criteria for feeling confident about a project they have done, criteria vastly different for the child than for an evaluating adult. Applying an adult standard to a child and then criticizing the child for their so-called failure to perform devalues that child.

Mocking

"You're fat! Look how fat you are!" Tammy had no more walked in the door of their house after clothes shopping when Eric started shouting those mean words to her. She knew he was mad she was the one who had gone shopping, while he was left at home. As he ran past her down the hallway, Eric snatched up the edge of her shirt, laughing, and tried to flip it over her head.

"Knock it off!" she yelled at him, furiously smoothing her new shirt back into place.

"Stop fighting!" Tammy's mother yelled from the kitchen, saying nothing about what Eric had said to her. Walking dejectedly to her room, Tammy knew Eric was right. She was fat. Looking at herself in her own bedroom mirror, the magic of her new shirt evaporated. At the store, the shirt had looked so lovely; she had looked so lovely. At home, Eric made sure to burst the bubble, as usual.

Tammy knew Eric didn't like her. Even though Eric was younger, he had a way of making Tammy feel smaller than he was. And he never got in trouble for it. Tammy sometimes caught their father snickering at Eric's comments, as though they were in on some secret joke, like how fat Tammy was. She knew it. She knew the shirt made her look terrible. She just had to figure how she could avoid wearing it after her mother had just bought it for her.

Emotional abuse happens when an adult makes fun of another person in a cruel or derisive way or allows others to do the same without objection.

Humor and levity are meant to make life enjoyable. But they should never be used at the expense of another, especially at the expense of a child. Laughter *with* others should never be confused for laughter *at* others. One uplifts, while the other puts down.

Lying

Whenever Keith thought about it, he tried his hardest not to become angry. He already knew his father wasn't coming for his birthday. His father had said it was about "the money," that he didn't have the money right then to make another trip out to visit. His father had told him how sorry he was and how he couldn't help it and he'd make sure to send something nice in the mail.

Keith had so wanted to believe what his father said was the truth this time. So often, it wasn't. But this time his father had seemed sincere and genuinely sad things hadn't worked out. Then his mother let slip that his father wasn't coming because he was taking his new girlfriend to Mexico. She was mad about the whole thing; Keith had heard his mother in her bedroom the other night complaining to Aunt Janet. Keith didn't want to be angry about it, but he was. He was angry most at himself for getting sucked up into another one of his father's lies. And he had no reason to wait for a gift to show up.

Emotional abuse happens when an adult does not act truthfully with a child with the intention of protecting themselves instead of protecting the child.

Naturally, adults are not able to share all information with children, who may be ill-equipped to deal with some of it. But children should still have as much explained to them as possible, factoring in their age and maturity level. Children should also not be purposefully lied to. When the truth does come out, as truth invariably does, the child can feel betrayed and experience anger, resentment, and frustration. When an adult perpetuates a pattern of lying, the child's sense of security is inverted. Instead of finding security in knowing the truth, the child gains a sense of security in accurately anticipating the lie. This creates a cynical, judgmental atmosphere that undermines adult authority.

Frightening

Rachel stood horrified in front of the mirror. One of her worst fears was happening. Her size 4 jeans were too tight. Rachel had so carefully lain down on the bed and slithered into them, knowing they were always snug after washing. But they were more than snug; they didn't fit anymore. Rachel could feel the tears of dread forming. This couldn't be happening! Frantically, Rachel went over what she'd eaten over the past few days. She'd been so very disciplined. Nothing fattening, well, except for that piece of pizza at youth group, but surely that couldn't be responsible. Or could it? One small slip and her size 4 jeans were in jeopardy. Furious, Rachel determined there would be no more slipups. She'd skip lunch and, if she got away with it, she'd find a way to beg off dinner too. Rachel was going to get herself back under control. Her mother had warned her again and again what happened to girls who let their figures go, how impossible it was to get them back later in life. That was never, ever, going to happen to Rachel, even if she had to starve herself to prevent it.

Emotional abuse happens when an adult transfers an inappropriate fear onto the heart of a child.

I've seen the scenario above played out time and time again, in varying circumstances, due to my work over the years with people with eating disorders. Fear of food, fear of getting fat, and fear of gaining weight are all anxieties adults can pass on to children, who are ill-prepared to test their veracity. I've seen adults pass fears of failure on to their children, burdening them with impossible standards of perfection. I've seen adults allow their agoraphobia to housebound their children. Children should grow up trusting in a world of possibilities instead of fearful of a world of assured catastrophes.

Withholding Promises

"But you said I could sleep over at Jeremy's house!" Nathan practically wailed his dismay.

"Don't you take that tone with me," his father warned. "I said you could sleep over if you did all of your chores."

"Which one didn't I do?" Nathan asked, going over in his mind the list on the refrigerator.

"I told you to clean out the garbage cans after they were picked up on Thursday. You didn't."

"When did you say that?" Now Nathan was really confused. "That's not on the list!"

"Of course it's not on the list. I told you to do it when you were mowing the lawn last Saturday."

"But," Nathan stammered, "I didn't hear you!"

"Well, you shook your head yes. It's not my fault if you didn't remember to write it down on the list."

"But I didn't hear you!" Nathan protested, with a sinking feeling it wasn't going to do any good. The fact was his father didn't have any intention of driving him over to Jeremy's. Nathan should have known his father would find a way to make not going his fault. When his father promised him something, there was always, what Nathan called, a backdoor. A way for his father to slip out of his promise if he wanted to and make it seem as though Nathan was to blame. How was he going to tell Jeremy? He'd promised.

Child abuse happens when an adult consistently makes promises but fails to keep those promises and blames the child for the failures.

Promises, which can be either straightforward or conditional, are a contract between people. A straightforward promise is "I will do A." A conditional promise is "If you do A, I will do B." Some adults have a pattern of only engaging in conditional promises. This way they have an "out," a way to blame the other person if they fail to uphold the promise. While this is irritating, at best, with adults, this behavior is abusive, at worst, with children.

Patterns of Emotional Abuse

With so many ways a child can be abused, some might ask if all childhoods, then, could be considered abusive at some level. And if all childhoods could be considered abusive, then wouldn't abusive just become another word for normal? This line of reasoning returns to the familiar illusion of normal and wasn't-so-bad. I appeal to you to avoid that trap.

As you consider your childhood experiences, please remember that childhood emotional abuse involves a consistent pattern of these demeaning, controlling, minimizing behaviors meant to rob a child of a healthy sense of self, of damaging their inherent dignity and self-worth. As you are looking for these patterns, please also remember that childhood emotional abuse can occur in a single, significant and traumatic event, where a child is left to feel marginalized, unworthy, unlovable, or damaged.

Above all else, childhood emotional abuse looks like pain and loss, like abandonment and grief, like fear and rejection. While these conditions can occur unintentionally in life because of life itself, the additional trauma of childhood emotional abuse is how, so often, this happens intentionally within families. Families are meant to provide children with love, acceptance, affirmation, and affection. Families are meant to be the nucleus of a child's sense of self-worth and value in the world. When families fail to provide this for the children, the children pay the price. When children pay the price, that's what childhood emotional abuse looks like.

5

The Violation of Neglect and Physical and Sexual Abuse

Emotional abuse is a violation of a child's sense of self, security, value, and worth. Tragically, children can be more than psychologically battered; they can be physically harmed through neglect, physical assault, and sexual exploitation. The scars of these experiences can run especially deep.

Lack of Care

The word *neglect* has a variety of meanings: (1) to pay no attention or too little attention to; disregard or slight; (2) to be remiss in the care or treatment of; (3) to omit, through indifference or carelessness; (4) to fail to carry out or perform; (5) to fail to take or use.[1] Sadly, I've been privy to the reality of these definitions in the lives of people I've worked with.

Ted grew up basically fending for himself. He was in the household but never felt part of it. Ted was an afterthought, a child born later than the others, expected to figure out how to get by because his parents were too old, too tired, and too demoralized about their own lives to care much about his.

Becky remembered spending far too many days inside. For one, she was told she couldn't go outside if her mother wasn't home, and her mother wasn't home most of the time. Also, sometimes, when Becky went outside, she had trouble breathing. She just couldn't run and play as hard as the other kids. When she got older, Becky learned she had asthma, which made her wheeze and hurt in her chest. She knew she could take medicine for the asthma, but she was told there wasn't any money for that. Becky was told as long as she didn't go outside, she wouldn't need the medicine.

Martin remembers how angry some of the other recruits were about having to sleep in bunks in dorms and get up at the crack of dawn. He used to laugh at their complaints and thought they were weak. Growing up, Martin always slept in a room with multiple siblings and cousins. There was never enough room; there was never enough quiet; there was never enough privacy. Sleep was something to be fought for; it never came naturally. Adults were always staying up late, talking, arguing, or just watching TV. And adults were always up early, getting ready, and rousting various kids out of sleep. When he was growing up, a restful night's sleep happened only when the adults were passed out.

Teri was scared. She'd gone with her sister to the store but not to buy something. They didn't have the money to buy anything. They went to the store to "take," not "steal" something. Teri's sister said it would be better if Teri took the box of feminine products because she was younger and wouldn't get into so much trouble if they got caught. Teri didn't understand why they had to take them, but her sister said their mother hadn't bought any and she needed them—right now. Besides, Teri's sister said she had better learn how to take the things she needed because that was the only way to be sure she got them.

Ben knew something was wrong when his teacher asked him to stay in class during recess. She wanted to know about the clothes he was wearing, which Ben thought was strange. They were just a blue shirt and jeans. She wanted to know how long he'd been wearing them and said she thought he'd been wearing them for the past three days. Ben was too embarrassed to tell her about the piles and piles of clothes that hadn't been washed. His mother was sick and hadn't done any washing. She was sick a lot—or tired or gone or said she just didn't want to. So, the clothes piled up. But he didn't say any of that to his teacher. He was scared he'd done something wrong and now she was asking questions. He'd make sure to go through the piles tonight and find the cleanest clothes for tomorrow. Maybe, from the front of the room, she wouldn't notice the smell.

Children can be neglected in many ways. The US government, which says neglect is the most common form of child mistreatment, defines the various forms of neglect this way:

Physical Neglect

- *Abandonment.* The government defines abandonment as leaving a child uncared for or unsupervised for more than two days.
- *Expulsion.* Expulsion is when an adult refuses to take custody of a child, kicks a child out of the home, or refuses to allow a child back into the home.
- *Shuttling.* Shuttling is the practice of leaving a child repeatedly in the care of others for extended periods of time, as in shuttling a child from place to place, from person to person, to provide care.
- *Nutritional neglect.* When a child is left hungry for long periods of time and/or is undernourished, this is considered nutritional neglect. Because of my work with eating

disorders, I've known people who were fed yet undernourished as children.

- *Clothing neglect.* Children require appropriate clothing
  for their needs. Their clothing should be clean, should fit
  them properly, and should match the season, such as warm
  coats, hats, and shoes for winter.
- *Other physical neglect.* This is the "other" category where
  the government puts actions like driving while intoxicated
  with a child in the car or leaving a child alone in a car.

Medical Neglect

- *Denial of health care.* The government's definition of denial of health care includes a great deal of legal language,
  but to me, this means not ensuring that children receive
  both the regular maintenance checkups needed as part of
  growing up, as well as the medical visits necessitated by
  childhood illnesses and injuries.
- *Delay in health care.* This includes not only medical care
  but also dental care. As a therapist, I would advocate adding mental health care.

Inadequate Supervision

- *Lack of appropriate supervision.* Caregivers of children
  must evaluate the age and maturity level of the child, the
  presence and/or intervention of other adults, how long
  and how often the child will be unsupervised, and the
  environment to determine what is appropriate.
- *Exposure to hazards.* This includes both in-home and
  outside hazards:
  » Safety hazards, such as poisons, choking hazards, elec-
    trical wires, stairs, the presence of drug paraphernalia
  » Smoking
  » Guns and other weapons

» Unsanitary household conditions, including rotting food, the presence of insect or rodent infestation, no running or clean water, the presence of human or animal waste in the home

» Lack of car safety restraints. I must say, this one caught me by surprise, having grown up with a generation of kids who often traveled without them. Safety restraints haven't been legally required that long—only since the mid-to-late 1980s.[2] Now that they are required, failure to provide them is considered neglect.

» Inappropriate caregivers. These people are defined as those unable to give care or who shouldn't be trusted to give care. Examples provided are young children giving care to other young children, someone who is a known child abuser, or someone with a substance abuse problem.

Environmental Neglect

• This type of neglect is leaving a child in an unsafe environment, such as a drug-infested neighborhood.

Emotional Neglect

• *Inadequate nurturing or affection.* This is defined as a pattern of inattention to a child's need for affection, emotional support, or attention.

• *Chronic or extreme spouse abuse.* This recognizes the damage done to children when they are exposed to severe and/or ongoing spousal abuse or domestic violence.

• *Permitted drug or alcohol abuse.* When caregivers passively allow or actively encourage the child to engage in alcohol or drug use, this is considered abuse.

• *Other permitted maladaptive behavior.* Caregivers who allow or encourage actions such as illegal activity or assaulting others are guilty of abuse. The example that comes to mind for me is parents who film their children physically assaulting other children.

- *Isolation.* Isolation involves denying children access to peers or other adults.

Educational Neglect

- *Permitted chronic truancy.* When caregivers allow children to be absent from school at least five days per month or fail to prevent them from doing so, they are guilty of permitted chronic truancy.
- *Failure to enroll or other truancy.* Truancy occurs when caregivers do not provide schooling for children, either through homeschooling, a private school, or a public school. This also includes allowing children to be gone from school for at least one month without a valid reason.
- *Inattention to special education needs.* Not all children have the same basic education needs. Some require remedial or specialized educational services. Failure to follow through with a diagnosed learning disorder constitutes childhood neglect.[3]

These lists represent research-based, government-documented horror stories. Behind the black-and-white definitions lie the pain and suffering of children caught in these conditions through no fault of their own and, sometimes, through no fault of their parents or caregivers. Adults are called on to make difficult choices where the care of children is concerned, and sometimes they take chances and make the wrong choice.

Taking all of this into account, as you look back on your childhood growing up, did you suffer neglect? Do you remember times when you were left alone, left in unsafe places, or left with unsafe people? Were you left without basic needs and had to fend for yourself or for others? If that is true, you experienced childhood abuse through neglect.

Physical Abuse

Children were not meant to be punched or kicked, beaten or bruised, burned or bitten as punishment. Children were not meant to be thrown up against walls or down stairs. They were not meant to be shaken violently or choked. Their hair was not meant to be pulled on or pulled out. Their bones were not meant to be broken. Their eyes were not meant to be blackened.

Children were not meant to be worked long hours or given physical tasks beyond their ability to perform. Children were not meant to be kept in small spaces, without adequate heat, light, or movement. They were not meant to be starved or undernourished as punishment. They were not meant to be deprived of sleep or hygiene to be taught lessons.

I believe physical child abuse is intentionally causing physical injury to children out of cruelty and disregard for the child. Even more distressingly, I believe physical abuse often happens because adults enjoy inflicting pain on children. They may deny it or attempt to blame the child, but I believe physical child abuse can invoke a twisted, perverse sense of control, relief, and even pleasure in some adults.

The realm of therapy defines an act called self-harm, where a person intentionally inflicts harm on themselves—through cutting, biting, burning, picking scabs, pulling hair, knocking their head against a wall or fists against a table, for example. The physical pain experienced by the person, in some way, masks or replaces the emotional pain that person is feeling. In self-harm, when the person feels psychological pain, they resort to an act of physical pain as a counterbalance. This act of physical pain is used as an inappropriate way to self-soothe or self-calm.

Some who physically abuse children use child-harm, instead of self-harm, to experience relief from their own psychological distress. If they're angry, they hit. If they're frustrated, they shake.

If they're irritated, they throw. If they're confused, they lock up. If they're tired, they assign work. If they're fearful, they withhold. The reason for the child-harm, then, has nothing to do with the actions of the child and everything to do with the distress of the abuser.

Were you physically abused? Were you hit or beaten, bruised or bitten or burned? Were you locked up for hours or days at a time? Were you conscripted into work that was too long and too hard for you to do? Were you someone's punching bag? Were you physically hurt as punishment for real or imagined wrongs? If so, my heart breaks for you because that is not the way a child should ever be treated.

Sexual Abuse

In a recent government report, 60 percent of reported sexual abuse cases involved children fourteen years or younger, and more than half of those were children under nine years old. The CDC (Centers for Disease Control) estimates that before the age of eighteen, 25 percent of girls and 16 percent of boys have been sexually abused.[4] Statistics may vary, but professional consensus appears to be that child sexual abuse is underreported, which makes those statistics even bleaker. The shame around child sexual abuse is pervasive and creates an extreme reticence to acknowledge it.

I believe sexual abuse occurs when adults engage children in activities of sexual content. Certainly, this includes individual or mutual acts of fondling, intercourse, or oral sex, where children take the place of consenting, sexually mature adults. However, I also believe sexual abuse happens when children are inappropriately sexualized. Randy experienced this when his father introduced him to pornography and encouraged him to participate in his father's pornography addiction when Randy was a young child.

As I said before, sexualization happens when children are encouraged and even rewarded for viewing or presenting themselves as sexually available, when they are not. One of the most disturbing examples of early sexualization in this country is the popularity of pageants and shows where small girls are dressed up, made up, and sexed up to mimic adult women, even movie stars, in very adult situations.

Children deserve the right to remain children until their natural maturation into sexuality. They deserve the right not to have their bodies molested or used for the sexual gratification of others. They deserve to be shielded from adult sexual behavior, for which they are unprepared. Failure to do these things not only robs children of their childhood but also warps their ability to experience healthy sexuality as adults.

Were you denied these rights as a child? Were you left unprotected from sexual content? Were you pushed into sexual activity? Did someone you trusted use you for their sexual satisfaction? Did that person's pleasure bring you suffering and pain? Did your experience leave you confused and vulnerable? Does a part of you still desperately want to keep the experience a secret? Are you still ashamed of what happened and blame yourself?

So much childhood abuse, of whatever type, happens when adults fail to take responsibility for the health and well-being of children. The responsibility lies squarely at the feet of the adult and never with the child. But tell that to the child. Tell that to the adult the child becomes. The shock waves of damage radiating from the abuse continue to batter that person's sense of self, security, value, and worth long after the experience is over. For the adult that child becomes, acknowledging that long-term damage can be as hard as acknowledging the abuse itself.

6

Childhood Abuse and Emotional Health

An abused child is an abandoned child in so many ways, as the child has been denied the love, care, and concern they have every right to expect from their caregivers. In situations of abuse, not only are love, care, and concern denied, but they are also often replaced by a true house of horrors, with no safety, no peace, and no trust. Such a dysfunctional formative environment creates a wave of damage that crashes into the processes of maturation and healthy development. In the presence of childhood abuse, whole-person health is compromised—emotional, intellectual, physical, relational, and spiritual health.

I have found children to be both fragile and resilient. Their resiliency is shown through their ability to hope, trust, and endure. Their fragility is shown through an incomplete understanding of adult motives, reasons, and objectives. Children so often find a way to navigate through life in the short term. To avoid a danger, they will skew off on a different path, without realizing the problematic trajectory of that temporary way out.

Sadly, when abuse is present, a child's healthy path through life is hijacked. The paths they should have traveled—the roads of trust, security, love, attention, appreciation, care, and concern—are cordoned off by the abuse. Instead, they are forced to travel down roads of fear, insecurity, hardship, frustration, anger, distrust, and chaos.

I am not surprised by the emotional damage of childhood abuse; I expect it. What continually surprises me is how those who have been abused as children—through creativity, ingenuity, and sheer force-of-will—still find their way to hope, love, forgiveness, and faith. But traveling through the negativity of abuse as children takes its toll; a toll that can become due and payable in adulthood.

Emotional Cost of Childhood Abuse

The damage abuse causes to a child's emotional health can seem overwhelming. My purpose in discussing the following emotional impacts is certainly not to contribute to an impression that overcoming childhood abuse is impossible. I retain my strong faith in the resiliency of the human spirit, the redemptive power of faith, the restorative power of forgiveness, and the reaffirming power of love. My purpose is to bring to light the emotional damage possible from childhood abuse so that you will understand you are not to blame. You have been damaged, but you are not defective and the damage can be repaired. To begin repairs, though, you need to recognize where and how to start.

Anxiety

Zoe caught herself hyperventilating, experiencing again that familiar sense of dread. Things were going too well. Zoe knew there was always a price to pay when things went too well. In fact, the more things went well in her life, the more Zoe became watchful for the pendulum to swing back into balance. The question wasn't if things would go wrong, but when. She made sure she always stayed on alert so she wouldn't be caught by surprise.

Abused children live in a world of dread. They also live in a world where they've learned they are responsible for their safety. In such a world, there is no standing down. They live on high alert—all the time. When these children find themselves responsible for other children, the sense of hyper-watchfulness is compounded. These children become tightly wound, emotionally stretched as they attempt to monitor their worlds for anticipated dangers. As such, they are highly reactive, twitching at the slightest movement or smallest sound. They default to a world of imminent disaster. Red alert becomes their familiar state, a known place of warped safety.

Did you grow up always wondering when the next shoe would drop, whether it was a harsh word, a taunt, a slap, or a touch? Where and when did you feel safe? Did you ever feel safe? High anxiety can be a way of coping with such a world. In a world where you are a target, you learn never to let your guard down, you keep it up, all the time, just in case.

Depression

Isaiah rolled over and looked at the clock. His first thought was, *Time to get up.* His second thought was, *Why? Why bother getting up at all?* He hadn't slept well; he never did. *Just call in sick,* he told himself, but even that seemed like too much trouble. If he didn't show up and didn't call, well, maybe he'd get fired. Then he wouldn't have to get up and get dressed and pretend he cared about going to work. Caring about anything was a trap. Things he cared about always got taken away.

As I've said, abused children are resilient. They are inventive and creative about finding ways to overcome and survive their abuse. Yet chronic abuse can take a significant toll on what I call "emotional buoyancy," that ability to spring back and recover from psychological trauma. A child may find that recovering a sense of emotional balance increasingly becomes more challenging with frequent and damaging psychological shocks. With childhood abuse, hope takes a beating. Bearing the weight of belief in a positive future can become a very heavy burden.

Did you grow up wishing for things that you knew, deep down, weren't possible? How did you feel when they didn't happen? Disappointed? Foolish for even thinking you could have them? Did you decide, at some point, it was just easier to expect the worst? And did expecting the worst make living life harder or easier? Were there times when you just wanted to run away, hide, and feel nothing at all? Did you grow up learning not to hope for things so you wouldn't be hurt? At least, that's what you told yourself.

Flashbacks

As the door to the elevator closed, Debbie heard a raised voice down the hallway. In that moment, she was no longer riding the elevator to the basement of the parking ramp to get to her car. Instead, in her mind, she was curled up in a ball inside her closet, hoping the voice in the hall wouldn't get any closer. Debbie didn't see the floor numbers slowly tick down. Instead, she heard the voice again, with that certain pitch he used—both angry and excited—coming closer. She had to hide, not that hiding ever did any good. When the elevator door opened and she heard the squeal of tires going around concrete corners, Debbie sprang up, confused about where she was. Thank God no one else was in the elevator with her. How could she possibly explain what she'd just lived through—again?

Abused children can have vivid memories of their abuse etched in their minds. These vivid memories can sometimes be triggered, years later, by seemingly innocuous things—a smell, a sound, a look, a touch. The trauma and fear of the past come rushing back, overwhelming the present. The person finds themselves awash in those sights, sounds, smells, feelings, and perceptions that were so damaging and, once again, so real.

Have you ever been transported back to a particularly painful or traumatic time? What triggered this experience? Was it a place? Do you now avoid such places? Was it a person? Do you now avoid that person? Was it a situation? Do you now avoid such situations? Are you terrified you can't control when and where it might happen again? Childhood abuse, though in the past, has the capacity to limit life in the present and future.

Dissociation

Phil walked into the conference and took a seat along the wall. He was already feeling spacey, like he did whenever he was stressed. He wanted, so much, to be anywhere else. Phil hated these "team" meetings with a passion; his cubicle was much safer. He survived these meetings by disconnecting, playing word games in his head, and praying no one asked him a question. Phil was very good at physically being in one place and mentally going to another. Such a skill was a necessity at one time; now he found it increasingly convenient.

Some people may not be familiar with the word *dissociate*. Dissociate is the opposite of associate. To associate means to connect things together. For example, you may associate the weekend with relaxation. To dissociate means to disconnect. When dissociation happens, in a psychological sense, a person can enter into a type of unreal, dream-like state where they experience events but are disconnected from them. Abused children can use dissociation to disconnect themselves mentally from an event of emotional or physical harm. Within a safe place in their mind, they attempt to shield themselves from fully experiencing that event.

I've heard this experience described by childhood abuse survivors as zoning out or as a type of out-of-body experience. Have you ever felt this way in times of stress? Have you ever lost track of where you were for a moment or more? Have you ever lost track of time? This dissociation is not some pleasant little daydream. The person is not running toward something out of boredom as much as running from something out of fear.

Lack of Self-Awareness

Holly looked at the list of options, bewildered. She'd never had to take a personality test before for a job. The questionnaire asked, "When I'm unable to do a job the way I want, I . . ." The options were: "(a.) get mad; (b.) get help from others; (c.) start over and try a different way; (d.) ask for another job." Holly had no idea how to answer. Timidly, she got up and asked the receptionist why the question was part of the interview. The woman smiled and explained, "That question has to do with self-awareness." Holly smiled back automatically, even though she had no idea what self-awareness was. Taking her seat again, she gave up answering the question and instead tried to figure out how to leave the interview.

Abused children may, as a survival mechanism, become quite adept at reading the emotional states of others. This knowledge is important to their safety, so they know when to run, when to hide, when to stay quiet, when to be submissive. They learn how to ride the emotional currents of their abusers. This outward focus on the emotional states of others can create a condition where they are less attuned to their own emotional states. In addition, if their emotional states continually are filled with fear, frustration, anger, or concern, they may intentionally distance themselves from their inner thoughts.

If you were asked how you feel about yourself, could you answer? Are you able to monitor how you feel and why you feel that way? Do you know what you value? Are you aware of how others view you? Are you surprised by how people view you? Are you afraid to ask? Is answering a question about your weaknesses easier than answering a question about your strengths? Self-awareness is how people keep themselves centered amid the push and pull of people, events, feelings, and knowledge. Accurate self-awareness can be difficult for survivors of childhood abuse because they were given a faulty image of themselves.

Low Self-Esteem

Rich checked the luggage in the trunk for the third time, just for something to do. He'd been dreading this day for more than a year. His son, Dean, was going off to college three hours away. Dean was everything a father could want and, frankly, the only decent thing Rich had. When Rich's marriage to Dean's mother didn't work out, he'd made sure to live just a few miles away so he could stay close to Dean. Rich considered Dean's life to be his life, especially through high school. Rich was nobody without Dean, Dean's friends, Dean's activities, Dean's popularity. Now, all that was ending. Dean was off to create a new life without him. Terrified, Rich knew his only positive identity was as Dean's dad, and without Dean, he was nothing.

An abused child can be knocked down (sometimes literally) every time they exhibit a healthy sense of self. These children are often taught by their abusers that they are not smart or good or valuable. They are taught their ideas are not worthwhile. They are taught their needs are not important, that they are not important. Without an internal sense of validation, abused children may look to others to fill that void. I've seen survivors of childhood abuse, like Rich, who gained their entire sense of value through their children or spouse, never through themselves. When that spouse or child left, for whatever reason, they found themselves completely adrift, without purpose, without value. They became empty, lacking a sense of who they were.

Were you made to feel worthless growing up? Were your accomplishments minimized or disregarded? Were you told you were to blame for the bad things that happened to you, that you deserved them because of who you were? Did it seem you could never do enough or be enough to gain praise or recognition? At some point, did you just stop trying? Did you start to believe you couldn't, wouldn't, or shouldn't ever measure up? Carrying such a devastatingly large burden of negativity from your childhood can make it exceedingly difficult for you to develop a positive self-image.

Isolation

Janice saw the call coming in, vacillated a second or two, and then clicked off the ringer. Part of her really wanted to take Kelly's call, but the other part of her won that battle; it usually did. Kelly was fun and active, with all kinds of ideas about things to do and places to go. Janice couldn't figure out why Kelly liked her and kept inviting her. Janice was usually tempted, but going out with Kelly meant getting dressed and putting on makeup and worrying about how she looked and who else was going to be there and where they were going and what she'd have to do. There were just too many unknowns. Janice knew exactly what she was going to do tonight; what she did every night. Just herself—no demands, no surprises.

Abused children often learn to fend for themselves; they become distrustful of others and find ways to fill their own needs. Sometimes abused children are left alone for long periods of time with no one to connect with but themselves. Sometimes, if the child feels the need to hide abuse, others become a danger to the must-keep secret. These situations damage a child's ability to understand and form healthy connections with other people—both peers and adults.

If given the choice between being with people or being alone, do you more often choose to be by yourself? Does being alone feel safer to you? Does adapting to other people—what they need or want from you—seem like too much trouble most of the time? Are you perfectly happy being by yourself, watching shows or playing on the internet? Would you rather text someone you know than be with that person? Abused children can learn that their zone of safety is quite small and only big enough to fit one.

Low Self-Confidence

Amanda was relieved that her presentation had gone well, when she knew it could have gone very differently. Luckily, David had helped with that last troublesome part. *Never again*, Amanda thought to herself as she gathered up the extra handouts and pens. She looked up and saw her supervisor entering the room, smiling. Cautiously, Amanda smiled back and listened, uncomfortably, to her supervisor praise her presentation. All Amanda wanted to do was get out of there. Then her supervisor mentioned that she thought corporate should see the presentation at the next semiannual meeting. Her supervisor left excited; Amanda felt nauseated.

As I've said before, abused children can feel as though they have a target on their backs. They are singled out and blamed for the harm that happens to them. Being noticed is a negative. When they were children, putting themselves "out there" could have resulted in further abuse.

Do you purposefully avoid situations where you might be the center of attention? Are you fearful of making yourself a target for the criticism or ridicule of others? Do you assume others won't like or appreciate what you've done? Do you assume people are judging you negatively, from what you say to what you wear to what you do? Are you more afraid of failing than afraid of not trying? Abused children, who often live in a chaotic world, have fewer markers for confidence in themselves, in others, and in how they are treated in and by that world.

Anger

Travis looked at the clock and took a deep breath. Eight minutes until the meeting with his lead. What now? Travis really didn't like the guy but had to pretend he did. He had to hide that dislike and bury it somewhere deep so he didn't lose his chance at a promotion. All that guy did was complain and tell him what he should have done. Just thinking about the meeting was making Travis upset. Travis couldn't get upset. If he got upset, the mask might come off. For two blissful minutes, Travis went over in his mind what he'd so love to say to the guy. Two minutes silently venting his anger and then six minutes to wrestle that anger under control.

As human beings, we are designed to react to pain with anger. In situations of childhood abuse, pain and anger become twisted. Children who are painfully abused may be punished for exhibiting anger at that natural pain. When children who are abused experience the anger of their abusers, they may learn to distrust anger, even their own. Abused children may be taught that anger is dangerous and something to be avoided at all costs. Or, abused children may be taught that anger is the preferred method of dealing with life. With such extremes, they have no example of how to deal with natural anger in a healthy, productive way.

When was the last time you remember getting angry? How angry were you? What were you angry about? How often are you angry at yourself? How often are you angry at others? Are you afraid of your anger? When you are angry, is it easy for you to figure out why you are angry? Have other people commented about your anger? Do you make sure no one knows when you're angry? Childhood abuse leaves a deep well of anger fed by the pain you experienced. Anger does not evaporate by pretending it doesn't exist. And venting anger, without understanding it, only keeps the well of anger full.

Perfectionism

Megan was furious. After all that time and energy she spent getting the house in shape, Chad just spit in her face. He didn't do that, literally, of course, but that's how she felt. Right there on the kitchen counter was the day's mail—some opened, some not. Her pristine counter was spoiled. And who did he expect to take care of the mail? Her, of course. She would have checked over the mail anyway because Chad never did it right. He was always failing to shred at least one piece of mail that could lead to identify theft. Nowadays, you couldn't be too careful. As her mother taught her, everything had a place and everything had to be in its place. When everything was in its place, there was safety; there was refuge. Megan deserved such moments of refuge, considering all the time and energy she spent making sure everything was done just right.

Abused children become the receptacle of all sorts of blame. In an attempt to control their situation, some children will try to attain perfection. If they can do everything right, then, perhaps, they won't be blamed. The analogy that comes to my mind is a greyhound race, where the greyhound runs around and around in circles, trying desperately to catch the unattainable rabbit. Of course, this analogy only goes so far. In actuality, trainers occasionally allow the greyhound to catch the rabbit or the greyhound will give up trying. Some children, in my experience, will continue trying, even when they never catch the rabbit.

Do you need things in your life to be a certain way to feel safe? Do you need people to act in a certain way to feel protected? Protected from what? Protected from whom? Do you demand perfection from yourself? Do you extend that demand to others? How do you feel when you fail? How do you feel when others fail? Is it more important to do that thing right than it is to be with other people? Is doing something right more important than doing something together? Perfectionism can perpetuate the abuse through the false belief that the unattainable is just within reach if only you try harder.

Fear of Failure

There Gabe went, talking about how he was going to fix up that car. Sometimes, that's all Gabe wanted to talk about, but he never did anything about it. Whenever Corey drove by Gabe's house, there was the junker, rotting away in the side yard, weeds growing up through the tireless wheel wells. Corey had been the one to haul it over to Gabe's house three years ago, because, back then, he'd believed Gabe meant to fix it. That's what Gabe had said, but that's all he had done—talk about it. Three years later, there it sat—rusting, unfixed. Corey wished Gabe would either fix the car or just shut up about it.

Childhood abuse can create a compulsion toward perfectionism in some children. That perfectionism coin, however, also has an opposite side. Some people believe perfection is possible and strive continuously to achieve it. Other people believe perfection is impossible and continuously avoid attempting it. If you believe you must be perfect to be safe, but you also believe such perfection is impossible to achieve, then safety becomes impossible to achieve. The only way to avoid failure, when success is defined as perfection, is to avoid starting the task in the first place.

Do you talk about what you're going to do but have trouble starting? Is it easier for you to envision what success looks like than accomplishing that success? Are you constantly disappointed by the results you achieve? When you start a project, are you excited or fearful about the outcome? How many unfinished "projects" do you currently have? Do you feel a sense of guilt or shame at the number of things you haven't started or finished? Being told as a child that you had to do more, be more, to be pleasing is a terrible burden. And when you tried as hard as you could but continued to fail, that burden just got heavier. Some children collapse under the weight and give up.

Acting Out Sexually

Brooke glanced across the room and saw Russell looking at her. She knew that look. Russell was interested, definitely. He was cute and a little shy. Brooke, having just broken up with Shaun, went to the party hoping Russell would be there. Brooke didn't want to be without a boyfriend; she needed a boyfriend to feel good about herself. As casually as she could, Brooke began to work her way over near where Russell was standing with two of his guy friends. If he found a way to detach from them, he was interested. Brooke was excited; dating was always a dance, trying to figure out what the other person wanted, and she was an excellent dancer.

An abused child spends a great deal of time either feeling out of control or desperately searching for a means of control. Being able to provoke a sexual response in another person can be a form of control. Children who have been sexually abused come to understand the power of sex, both to hurt and to control. They may use sex to gain control over people and situations. Children who have been psychologically or physically abused may use sex to "purchase" affection, attention, or a warped view of love from another person. Children who have been neglected may use sex to fill up the emotional voids in their lives.

How do you feel about your sexuality? Do you feel your relationships are healthy sexually? Are you ashamed of ways you've traded sexual activity for attention or affection? Do you feel you must be willing to engage in sex to maintain a relationship? Do you think sex is something you give or something you do? Childhood abuse compromises fundamental human relationships, including sexual relationships.

Sexual Avoidance

Alex laughed and told Jerry he wasn't interested in going; he had to put in OT at work on Saturday, so a late Friday night just

97

wasn't in the cards. Because he and Jerry worked together, Alex now had to be sure he went in for at least a couple of hours, which wouldn't be bad. He'd mess around and get some work done. Anything to avoid one of Jerry's parties. Alex had gone once and found himself in way over his head. Couples were forming everywhere and that made Alex very uncomfortable. Would he be expected to "couple up"? Alex wasn't interested in that. The thought of someone getting that close to him wasn't, in any way, appealing. Letting someone get that close wasn't safe.

Tragically, in many instances, a child's sexuality is stolen by a person of trust. Children who have suffered abuse can have difficulty navigating a healthy sexual balance later in their lives and relationships. Some swing to the side of promiscuity and unsafe sex. Others swing the opposite way and forgo sexual relationships altogether. If sexual situations with others are deemed unsafe, they may be drawn to pornography and self-gratification. Childhood sexual abuse causes barriers in adulthood to understanding and forming healthy sexual relationships.

Do you distrust the physical intimacy of others? Are you in a sexual relationship but feel disconnected from it, like you're just going through the motions? Have you decided it's better, safer to avoid relationships where intimacy might be expected? Does the thought of letting someone get that close to you cause apprehension, fear, or shame? Does such a risk not seem worth the trouble? Abused children often must put up emotional barriers out of fear of being hurt. Those barriers may remain strong and in place well into adulthood.

Psychosomatic Conditions

Wendy was frustrated. Didn't they know she couldn't walk that far? They were family; they should have known better. Wendy had always had a "delicate" condition. Of course, Wendy's mother always said she was just looking for attention, which her mother was too busy to give. Mama never believed Wendy when she explained she couldn't do things, but Papa did. He would cuddle Wendy close and tell her she was going to be okay and she could stay with him. Wendy remembered her parents arguing about her, with Mama saying she was lazy and Papa saying she was delicate. Wendy liked being called delicate much more than she liked being called lazy.

Abused children who are neglected or marginalized sometimes find ways to attain attention, even negative attention. Some children may seek to establish their identity by claiming physical conditions or illnesses. In addition, childhood abuse carries its own burden of psychological distress, which can manifest as physical ailments. The heart is sick, so is the body. Over time, of course, the risk is that imagined illnesses become real ones.

Do you suffer from aches and pains that fail to show up on tests? Have you been to doctor after doctor only to be told they "can't find anything wrong"? Are you left feeling discounted and not believed? Does this make you even more convinced that something is wrong? Are you frustrated that family and friends don't show appropriate sympathy for what you're going through? Psychological trauma creates physical symptoms that can be misunderstood by a child, leading to confusion well into adulthood.

Unrealistic Guilt

Ron slammed on the brakes, but not in time. Shaken up, he looked over at Sharon, who was checking the back seat to make sure Daniel was okay. Taking a deep breath, Sharon assured him Daniel looked fine; the airbags hadn't even deployed. Cautiously, Ron got out of the car to check on the other driver. The man immediately apologized and said he hadn't seen the stop sign. He wanted to know if everyone was okay and Sharon said they seemed to be, as she got Daniel out of the car seat and handed him to Ron. Ron was relieved Sharon was going to handle the other driver. He held on to Daniel and relived the accident in his mind. Sharon was probably going to blame him, even though she clearly was telling the other driver the accident was his fault. It wasn't. Ron knew he should have seen the other car coming. He should have stopped. Devastated, Ron knew it was his job to protect his family and he'd failed. There was no way Sharon was going to let him off the hook for such a failure.

Abused children are conditioned to believe they are responsible for the bad things that happen. They are programmed to accept blame and guilt. This assumption of guilt can come automatically because of that abusive environment. This assumption of guilt, in some ways, creates security for an abused child through a perverted sense of control. They think, *If I am to blame, then I am responsible. If I am responsible, then maybe I can find a way to make things better next time. I will take the blame so I can feel in control.*

Can you relate to those "I" statements? Have you felt that way? Do you find that you assume you are responsible for problems that arise? Are you used to wearing that shroud of guilt? Has it become a comfortable garment for you? Do you feel somewhat naked and exposed to the world without it? Realistic guilt accepts appropriate responsibility. Unrealistic guilt appropriates all responsibility. Abused children have been taught there is only one type of guilt—theirs.

Crisis-Oriented

Jacqueline sprang into action after hearing Brandy's concern. *Oh no, Brandy,* thought to herself, *here she goes.* Brandy almost didn't say anything to her mother, but she was afraid she would hear about it from someone else because Jacqueline was tied in at

Brandy's school and knew all the other moms. Jacqueline barely let Brandy finish explaining the problem before she went into what Brandy secretly called "Mom's crisis mode." Truthfully, Brandy sometimes enjoyed watching her mom take off after someone or something that had given Brandy a problem. Brandy also knew sometimes her mom went overboard. She hoped this wasn't going to be one of those times.

Abused children can spend a great deal of their growing up years in crisis mode. This becomes the "normal" state of being and, thus, very familiar. Some children grow up with parents who are incapacitated, through substance abuse or mental or chronic illness. These children can be called on to take care of the adult instead of the other way around, acting *in loco parentis*. In such crisis situations, the child is forced into a position of responsibility and control. The child may receive attention and appreciation for acting in this inappropriate role. They may also gain a sense of value through these crises and seek to replicate them later in life to feel worthy.

Are you a "fixer"? Do you feel compelled to rush in and solve other people's problems? Do you believe you are the best person to solve an issue? Does being in a crisis make you feel needed? Do you have an unusual sense of clarity when responding to urgent need? Are you afraid your value as a person comes only from your ability to problem-solve? Do you anticipate crises and feel a sense of relief when called on to address one? Crises are times of heightened emotional and physiological response. The chemicals involved in fight-or-flight or tend-or-befriend responses are powerful, and some people develop a type of addiction to them.

Substance Abuse

Kenny had learned to be very careful. He'd started out stealing small amounts of his father's liquor. He knew which types he could cut with water without being detected. After the divorce, he started stealing the pot his mom's boyfriends brought into the house. If he was careful, and didn't get too greedy, he could snatch away a bit here and there until he had enough for his own joint. Of course, there was that time he got impatient and took a full joint. He got caught, and that didn't turn out well for him. Growing up, Kenny figured out how to get what he wanted and to be careful about it. Now that he was older and had a job, it was harder because of the mandatory drug testing. That hadn't made him quit. No, it just meant he had to become even smarter.

Abused children live a stressful, painful life. To alleviate their suffering, some turn to substances, such as alcohol or prescription or illicit drugs. These substances may be readily available in their abusive environments, increasing the temptation to use them. In some cases, abused children may be encouraged by their abusers to partake of these substances. Abusers may use these as "rewards" for compliant behavior by those they abuse. In any case, these children are exposed to powerful substances without an adult understanding of their long-term effects.

Do you regularly use substances to cope with stress? What about to numb out and forget your problems? Have you told yourself you need to cut down or quit but have been unable to do so? Are you afraid of what your life would be like if you couldn't use? When did you first start using? What were the reasons then? What are the reasons now? Substances can be used to mask psychological trauma and distress, but they can have long-term, detrimental effects that do nothing to alleviate the pain.

Eating Disorders

Jillian looked around her room at all the boxes piled in the corner and felt an urge to weep. She wanted to but she wouldn't. There was no point in crying; that wouldn't solve anything. Nobody asked her about the divorce. Nobody asked her if she wanted to move to a different state. Nobody asked her anything. She was supposed to shut up and do what she was told; the only person allowed to cry was her mother. Jillian could still remember how she'd felt when her mother told her the divorce was final and about the move. Jillian had started to cry and then her mother had started to cry and told her not to. It wasn't fair. Jillian had to leave her school and her friends and she wasn't to cry about it. Fine, she'd make the best of it. A new school, new friends, a time to reinvent herself. She had all summer to lose weight so she could start high school thin. Then she wouldn't have to worry about finding friends; friends would find her. She wouldn't cry or complain; she'd do what she needed to do—whatever it took.

Abused children are often not allowed to respond to trauma or traumatic events in appropriate ways for children. They are expected to act as "little adults." Sometimes wounded adults call on them to take on the role of comforter or companion. They are expected to disregard their own needs and fulfill the needs of others. In some abused children, this unrealistic expectation and disregard of their feelings produce feelings of anger and rage. If these reactions are also quashed, the anger and rage must find a substitute outlet. In some abused children, this expression leads to an eating disorder. The child may begin to control body weight as a way to control at least one thing in their life. That control of their body may come in the form of restriction, in anorexia; of bingeing and purging, in bulimia; or in a preoccupation with weight and image, in body dysmorphia. Some abused children seek out the comfort of food and engage in binge eating but without any purging, resulting in more and more weight gain.

Are you consistently thinking about how you look? What you eat? Do you experience a sense of satisfaction when you reach certain weight goals? Have you disregarded the concern of others over your eating patterns or your weight? Do you feel you deserve to be thin? Do you feel you deserve to be fat? Is food the one comfort, the one sure thing in your life? Food is a mood modifier and can be used—either by undereating or overindulgence—as a way to cope with psychological stress.

Self-Harm

Marcus pressed the tip of the knife into the flesh of his forearm, watching in fascination as the blood pooled up around the puncture and spilled over. He moved his arm back and forth, creating a pattern to the blood. He only did small punctures on his forearm. If he felt he needed to cut deeper, he used the same spot in the underarm curve of his bicep. Deep enough to hurt and bleed but shallow enough to avoid the muscle, which he was very proud of. When other guys said he was "cut," he always laughed. They thought they were talking about his build, but he knew the truth. The truth was he relished these times of release. He had given himself permission to think about the pain and beatings of the past, when he'd had no control over the blood he'd spilled. He did now. When he bled, it was on his terms—no one else's. Never again.

Abused children carry the pain of their abuse with them, often without an outlet to express their hurt, shock, distress, or anger. Just as an eating disorder is a way to express that distress, so is the act of self-harm. In self-harm, a person uses physical pain to try to alleviate psychological pain. Self-harm includes cutting but also can be manifested in hitting one's head against a hard surface, punching one's fist through a door or wall, pulling out hair, creating and/or picking scabs, and burning one's skin with a curling iron or cigarette. The pain of the injury is used to substitute for the pain kept walled up inside.

Have you ever intentionally injured yourself just to experience how it felt? Did you experience a sense of relief? When you're distressed, do you find yourself seeking distraction through pulling your hair or poking your skin? Would you rather experience a temporary physical pain instead of an ongoing distress because of something you have no control over? Have you ever scared yourself over how much injury you were willing to inflict on yourself to feel better? Psychological pain lies deep in the soul and cannot be exorcised by physical means; the only outcome of such self-harm is more harm.

My Purpose

Please allow me to reiterate at the end of this chapter what I said at the beginning: the weight of damage done to emotional health by childhood abuse can seem overwhelming. My purpose in discussing these emotional impacts is certainly not to contribute to an impression that overcoming childhood abuse is impossible. I retain my strong faith in the resiliency of the human spirit, the redemptive power of faith, the restorative power of forgiveness, and the reaffirming power of love. My purpose is to bring to light the emotional damage possible from childhood abuse so that those of you who suffer will understand you are not to blame.

An additional purpose is to bring to light difficulties you may be experiencing in your life for which you have been unable to determine a cause. It is my hope that, after reading through these possible effects, you are able to discover a link between some confounding behaviors you experience now to trauma or abuse in your past. And, having identified such a potential connection, you will find motivation to explore additional ways to recover and create change.

7

Additional Costs of Childhood Abuse

The emotional costs of childhood abuse are significant, but regrettably, they are not the only costs. The long-term effects often manifest later in life and are, therefore, difficult to connect back to the events of an abusive childhood. In addition, the cumulative effects of emotional trauma may take years to reach critical mass.

The emotional impacts of childhood abuse create physical, relational, and spiritual consequences. There is a definite connection between what the mind conceives and what the body experiences. People are linked through their relationships with one another. Understanding meaning and purpose amid life experiences is a spiritual endeavor. In the whole-person model—integrating one's emotional, intellectual, physical, relational, and spiritual health— damage to one part of the whole person ricochets into the other parts of the whole person.

Physical Effects of Stress

Kayla barely made it into her office before she started pacing, breathing hard, and thinking even harder. She was sure she'd heard Larry talking to Mark about her. Even though Kayla didn't exactly hear what Larry was saying, she knew it couldn't be good. Mark was after her job; she knew it. Frantically, Kayla thought back over her job performance. Was there any reason she could be blamed for something? If there wasn't, Kayla still knew Mark could make up something. Her job wasn't safe; she wasn't safe. Kayla paced in her office, knowing she would have to protect herself from attack. She could do that; she'd learned how to do that early in life.

One of the biggest culprits, I believe, of lingering physical effects from childhood abuse is stress. Children who have been abused experience physical and emotional distress and trauma. The physical damage may mend and heal, but the emotional reaction to this trauma often remains active and forceful. Fear, uncertainty, anger, and frustration can be the by-products of abuse that don't fade but instead build over time. A person in constant stress mode sees danger everywhere and security nowhere. A person under stress is a reactive person who may not wait to consider the full situation—a condition of shoot first, ask questions later.

Do you try to forget the abuse you suffered as a child because of how it makes you feel? Does thinking about those times cause your heart to race, your palms to sweat, your hands or feet to tingle? Do you find yourself going into high-stress mode even when others don't exhibit the same level of concern? Do you sometimes feel yourself threatened by circumstances or other people? Once the danger has passed, is it harder for you than for others to come down from that heightened sense of alert? Does it feel better or safer to be on alert rather than relaxed?

The body's response to stress is an all-hands-on-deck call to action for physical systems, meant as a short-term answer to danger.

Living in stress-mode for the long term creates a physical drain on those systems, which can lead to physiological difficulties later in life. Working with survivors of childhood abuse, I've seen physical conditions I believe are derived, in part if not all, from a continuation of heightened stress. This belief, which I've developed over thirty-plus years of counseling, appears validated by research. A recent UCLA study published online in 2013 by the *Proceedings of the National Academy of Sciences* found that "searchers suggest that toxic childhood stress alters neural responses to stress, boosting the emotional and physical arousal to threat and making it more difficult for that reaction to be shut off,"[1] Children who have been abused enter a state of stress and distress, which changes the way their brains react to circumstances and stresses later in life. They become hardwired to hyper-react and have a difficult time standing down.

The American Psychological Association lists a cornucopia of negative health effects due to stress, such as muscle tension; headaches, asthma attacks; rapid breathing leading to panic attacks; cardiovascular problems; hypertension; inflammation of the circulatory system; higher cholesterol levels; increased epinephrine and cortisol levels; adrenal fatigue; insulin resistance and Type 2 diabetes; heartburn; gastrointestinal distress; irritable bowel syndrome; erectile dysfunction; irregular, painful, or absent menstruation; increased menopausal hot flashes; and reduction in sexual libido.[2] Because of the close connection between *what* we experience and *how* we feel, those who have survived childhood abuse need to be aware of the potential for health problems today to be linked to abuse from the past.

Relational Effects

If you grew up hearing that you were worthless, a bother, a mistake, not enough, how would you feel about yourself? If you were routinely beaten and blamed, how would you feel about yourself? If you were left to fend for yourself, treated as invisible or discarded, how would you feel about yourself? If you were used as a sexual outlet for another, how would you feel about yourself? The answers may be different for different people, but the overarching answer to each of those questions is "not good." Not feeling good about yourself damages the one relationship that serves as the foundation for all your other relationships—the relationship with yourself. Is it any wonder, then, that childhood abuse has the capacity to negatively affect your relationships later in life?

In the last chapter, I went over an extensive list of ways a person can be emotionally damaged by childhood abuse. Each of these ways (anxiety, depression, flashbacks, dissociation, lack of self-awareness, low self-esteem, isolation, low self-confidence, anger, perfectionism, fear of failure, acting out sexually, sexual avoidance, psychosomatic condition, unrealistic guilt, crisis-oriented, substance abuse, eating disorders, and self-harm) undermines a healthy relationship with self. And each of them can severely compromise relationships with others, from spouses to parents to children to friends to coworkers. When you don't feel good about yourself, your ability to feel good about others is adversely affected.

Codependency and Relationship Addiction

Antonio waited outside the store in the car, trying not to be impatient. Tara would be out soon enough, though she often talked about how she and her friends would laugh and joke and gab after work. Sometimes he'd have to take Tara and her friends to their favorite bar and wait while they had drinks together. He was expected to drive but never really was invited to be part of the group. That was okay, Antonio reminded himself. He'd do anything for Tara, anything to keep her happy, to keep her with him. Antonio knew he wasn't handsome or smart or successful or much of whatever else. He'd never won anything or been chosen for anything and now Antonio questioned daily why Tara had chosen him. His life had become hers. If he lost her, where would he be? Antonio waited in the car and tried not to think about that.

I believe one of the relational costs of childhood abuse is a tendency, in some survivors, toward codependency and relationship addiction. Dr. Tim Clinton, president of the American Association of Christian Counselors, and I recently wrote an entire book on this subject titled *Don't Call It Love: Breaking the Cycle of Relationship Addiction*. I first heard the term codependency through Melanie Beattie's work in her book *Codependent No More*. Developed through experiences with those in relationship with alcoholics, codependency has come to describe a relationship where one person believes their value emanates solely through another person To safeguard that relationship, the codependent person becomes obsessed with controlling the other person, often through enabling the other person's addictive behaviors. What began as a way to understand those in relationship with alcoholics has expanded to include other types of addictive behavior. For example: If you love me and stay with me, I'll help you continue to drink (or do drugs or eat too much or shop excessively or gamble or emotionally or physically abuse me).

A person whose self-value has been damaged or destroyed by childhood abuse may be especially susceptible to deriving worth and validation through another person. Unfortunately, some individuals will take advantage of such vulnerable survivors and seek to enter into a codependent relationship to exploit the survivor emotionally, physically, sexually, financially, or any or all of the above. These manipulative predators do not attempt to elevate the survivor's self-esteem but, rather, seek to depress it even further to gain the survivor's active agreement and participation in their addiction. They gain a sense of gratification merely from the power

111

and control they can exert over other people. These are exactly the type of people who would abuse a child, so the personality can be very familiar.

Codependency turns into relationship addiction when the object for self-validation is not a specific person but a codependent relationship. Thus, a person may end up in an addictive cycle of pursuing a relationship, establishing a relationship, attempting to control that relationship, strangling the relationship, being in fear of losing that relationship, losing the relationship, and starting the cycle all over again with someone else. I've had both men and women in my office mystified by their pattern of behavior concerning relationships, especially romantic relationships. They will say things such as, "I always seem to pick the wrong person," or "Why can't I ever find someone I can be truly happy with?" Real answers are possible when they stop looking at the other person and start looking at themselves.

Please don't interpret what I've said to mean that a person who has suffered childhood abuse will automatically enter a codependent relationship or become relationship addicted. Many survivors enter relationships with psychologically healthy individuals. And even psychologically healthy individuals are in no ways perfect. Anyone who enters a relationship with another person brings past baggage that can complicate things. But childhood abuse is extremely heavy baggage to carry into a relationship.

What is your pattern with relationships? Do you put up with harmful or hurtful behavior to stay in the relationship? Are you afraid of what will happen if you object? Are you worried no one else will love you? Do you take more pride in *whose* you are than in *who* you are? If you have been abused, if you have been abandoned or neglected, your psychological resiliency about who you are and your value and worth have taken a beating. You will need to be aware of how that damage is affecting your relationship with yourself and your relationship with others.

Parental Authority

Marnie was scared. She couldn't believe how mad she'd gotten at the kids just now. She felt like a stranger, watching herself unleash on them over something stupid. She'd told herself to stop, that they were just kids, but she hadn't been able to. The words and the anger just kept pouring out. Thank God, she hadn't hit any of them, though at one point she'd really wanted to. That's when she'd felt herself snap out of it. Dear God, how could she even have thought to do such a thing? Marnie had looked down at those two terrified little faces and, suddenly, saw herself looking back. She knew what that felt like. What was wrong with her? How had she ever let herself get so out of control? *Dear God*, Marnie thought, *what if it happens again and I can't stop? Who am I? Who have I become?*

As you consider the effect of childhood abuse on your relationship with others, I ask those of you who are parents, or who have access or authority over children, to give thought to how those relationships may be affected. Do you find yourself doing or saying things you swore you would never do or say when you grew up? Or do you find yourself giving in to childish requests and behaviors to avoid conflict? Would you rather say yes, when you really should say no, all to avoid a confrontation? Do you find yourself trying to be a "nice" parent more than a "good" parent?

If the parenting model you grew up with was fundamentally flawed, you may be at a loss to determine what is normal and what is not, what is helpful and what is harmful. You may go to the opposite extreme to avoid any semblance of harsh behavior. You may be terrified of becoming a monster yourself. You may gain satisfaction from finally being the one in charge. I implore you not to shy away from examining your own beliefs and behaviors about raising children, especially when it comes to discipline.

Other Relationships

Childhood abuse touches on all a person's relationships. If you were abused by one parent, how you feel about the other parent is touched. Are you angry the person didn't protect you? Are you sad because that person was abused too?

If you have siblings who were also abused growing up, how do you feel about them? Are you closer because of the abuse or do you tend to distance yourself from one another so you won't have to remember? Do you place blame on one of your siblings for your abuse? Do any of your siblings blame you?

If you have siblings who weren't abused, but you were, how do you feel about them? Are you angry at them because you were the one singled out? Did any of them "pile on" and participate in the abuse in one form or another? Does it matter if they were younger or older than you?

When you are making friends, do you avoid certain types of people because of how they make you feel? Are you drawn to other types of people because you feel they are safer? Do you avoid friendships altogether, considering them unsafe? Do you tend to lose yourself in your friendships, always trying to please?

On the job, do you have difficulty with authority? Do you immediately distrust certain people? Do you find yourself angry and confrontational with authority or do you find yourself wanting to remain invisible? Do you automatically assume coworkers are critical of you and the job you do? Does this make you afraid or defensive?

Your relationships as a child set the stage, if you will, for all relationships going forward. You are who you are, in part, because of the experiences you've had. When those experiences include childhood abuse, they leave an indelible stamp on how you view relationships, how you conduct yourself in relationships, and how you view other people.

Spiritual Effects

Father's Day at church. Graham dreaded the "celebration" this year. He'd found a way out of it last year, but with Ethan being born, Lauren certainly wouldn't allow that this year. Graham tolerated church for Lauren's sake but, truthfully, got some good out of the sermons and really enjoyed the young couples who went there. The people at church were fine; Graham just had a problem with God and the Heavenly Father thing. Graham's father hadn't been, in any way, heavenly. Graham figured it was best to give God a wide berth in case he was anything like his earthly father. Graham hoped God wasn't, but he just wasn't ready to take the risk.

Over the years, I've struggled to help people cope with an image of God as a super father figure. People come to me with problems relating to their earthly fathers. Perhaps they were emotionally distant or unnecessarily harsh. They may have been unyielding or overindulgent. When an earthly father is abusive, this creates a spiritual challenge for the child, who is told that God is their heavenly Father. While this description is meant to give the child reassurance, for abused children, this description can terrify. When an earthly father uses their authority to violate a child, that child's perception of God's authority can become suspect.

I have found abused children, as adults, have a variety of reactions to God:

- Some abused children understand God as their only refuge amid the abuse. They cling to God and credit him for saving them during their fragile childhood. Their relationship with God is strong.

- Other abused children feel like Graham and are suspicious of God. This negativity may be subtle, a refusal to engage God to any great depth or degree. Their relationship with God is shallow.

- Some abused children are openly angry at God. They accept that God is all-knowing and all-powerful and, within that context, believe God knew what was happening to them and failed to protect them. They blame God as well as their abuser. Their relationship with God is hostile.

- Other abused children are afraid of God. They believe in their total unworthiness and seek to please God, while also believing they can never succeed. Yet just as they tried to please their abuser to no avail, they continue to attempt to please God. Their relationship with God is fearful.

Additional difficulty arises if the abuser used spirituality or invoked God as a rationale for all or part of the abuse. Sadly, childhood abuse does happen in faith-based families. Because our clinic is faith-based, we have people who come for treatment specifically because they have a religious or spiritual background. Many of them were raised within a religious household. Tragically, in some of those households, children were taught they were flawed, worthless, and unlovable by God. They were taught they had to be perfect for God to accept them. They were told they could try and try and try, but never meet God's standard. Condemnation was taught and modeled. Love was dangled out in front of their hearts like some sort of prize to be won for good behavior, as determined by the parent. The parent became the proxy for God and constantly voted against the child.

At our clinic, we routinely ask those who are leaving treatment to complete a feedback survey. We want to know what we are doing right and what things we can improve on. The very last question on the survey over the years has been something to the effect of "tell us anything else you think we should know." I've been struck by the number of times people have, without prompting, related that one of the biggest components to their recovery has been a discovery or rediscovery that God loves them.

I am saddened that this simple biblical concept of "God loves me" gets warped and obscured by human failings. I am reminded of Jesus speaking to his disciples about the kingdom of God. For this heady theological discourse, Jesus used the example of a small child, whom he called into the middle of the discussion. Pointing to the child, he told the disciples, "If anyone causes one of these little ones—those who believe in me—to stumble, it would be better for them to have a large millstone hung around their neck and to be drowned in the depths of the sea."[3] God cares about children and the faith children innately have in him. Abuse can damage or destroy that precious faith.

How is your faith in God? Which relationship previously mentioned best describes your current relationship with him? Was it always that way? Would you like your relationship with God to be different? If so, in what way? Do you have children? What have you taught them about God? What has your life modeled about God?

As I have said, I believe children harbor a deep capacity for faith. I have seen how faith can take a beating because of childhood abuse. I confess, after hearing stories from survivors of childhood abuse, I have envisioned a millstone wrapped around certain necks. But anger and revenge are not my job; forgiveness and reconciliation are. My privilege over the years has been to watch many people find their way back to faith, to trust in God, and, ultimately, to forgiveness.

Whole-Person Effects

As I've tried to explain in these last two chapters, the cost of childhood abuse can be significant, affecting emotional, physical, relational, and spiritual aspects of a person's life. The stress triggered by the trauma can become an engrained response into adulthood, leaving a legacy of distress, distrust, and fear. Researchers

117

are diving deeper into the wide-ranging negative consequences of childhood abuse and improving our collective understanding. In some ways, adding to the list of negative outcomes can be discouraging. However, I have witnessed people finally uncover a reason for why they think, feel, and act, especially in harmful ways. Knowing the reasons gives a starting point for finding a solution.

8

Steps to Emotional Healing

Paula reluctantly came for couples' counseling. Her reason for even showing up, she told me, was because she'd put twenty-plus years of her life into the marriage and she wasn't going to let her husband's behavior screw that up. Paula didn't believe in divorce, considering it a failure, and she didn't tolerate failure. While no one is perfect, and her husband, Will, had his own issues, Paula clearly became the focal point of our sessions. She was rigid in her thinking, intolerant of anything she considered failure, and had extreme difficulty seeing or accepting her own part in their problems. Paula didn't just reject responsibility; she hurled it from her vicinity with amazing vehemence. She was not to blame; their marriage issues were really Will's issues; fixing him would fix the marriage. Paula knew exactly how he needed to be fixed but was at a loss about how to convince him to do things her way, hence the counseling. Paula had a professional opinion and expected me, the professional, to agree with her assessment. The whole thing almost blew apart when I didn't.

Healing emotionally from childhood abuse is not as simple as applying a splint to a broken heart. No lab test can determine thirty-year-old effects of psychological damage. No pill has been formulated to block negativity in the soul of an abused person. Healing is a difficult and painful process that takes place over time, with small leaps forward amid slips and falls and backward steps.

Healing requires patience, perseverance, and, I've found, a dogged determination to plow ahead, even when right now feels lousy and the future doesn't look any better. That's where Paula's husband was when we started the couples' counseling. Fortunately, for both of them, he didn't let that stop him. His love for Paula, their children, and their life together motivated him to keep moving forward toward healing, recovery, and reconciliation.

I've found that healing from childhood abuse follows a progression. Not everyone I've worked with travels down this path at the same pace or even at the same sequence but, at some point, each person touches the following markers along their healing journey.

Stop Running

It soon became clear to me that Paula's rigidity was not only directed at Will. She was astonishingly rigid about herself, her children, and her work. Once, I asked how she characterized a "loose end." Paula retorted that loose ends were things that could "hang you." She was even less complimentary of surprises, as Will related a fortieth birthday celebration that had gone disastrously wrong. So much of Paula's energies, I found, seemed to be focused on locking down control over her life, from what she wore to work to where they went on vacation to how the kids did in school. I began to ask myself why and suspected, as the adage goes, "An odd reaction is an old reaction."

Paula's incessant and long-standing need for control indicated to me a person whose life had felt out of control. I suspected that, in order to compensate for that time of extreme instability, Paula attempted to wrap herself in as much security as she could get, with security equating to control over people and events. The flaw in that strategy, of course, is the impossibility of truly controlling other people, events, or even yourself. Paula tried to control everything to feel secure, but never truly being in control, she never felt secure and had to keep trying, keep striving, keep moving to attempt to control the next thing and the next and the next.

Paula was running from something, something she didn't want to acknowledge. People run from all types of things, usually painful things. Paula's way to run from pain was through control, but others use alcohol, drugs, perfectionism, gambling, gaming, food, pornography, work, shopping, or relationships. You name it and someone, somewhere, has tried to use it as a way to cope with, run away from, or numb the pain.

The thing about running as a strategy is you have to keep running. You can never rest, never slow down, never drop your guard. That was Paula, and it was driving her family away. And, over the years, Paula was finding the effort harder and harder to maintain. To heal, she needed to stop running and face what she was running from.

Accept the Past

Paula experienced a psychologically abusive childhood where she and her brother were pitted mercilessly against each other for their father's approval. Praise from their father was the elusive prize and the siblings chose different ways to win. Paula's brother, Roy, was the deceiver. Three years older, Roy figured out how to undermine Paula's attempt to please their father to maintain his firstborn, superior status. Paula strove to be the perfect child—always compliant, always doing the right thing. The problem was Roy had a way of twisting the right thing Paula tried to do into something wrong. If that didn't work, Roy would lie.

Paula grew up in a household where truth didn't matter; only the perception of truth mattered and only the perception of one person mattered. Truth became not what you knew but what you could prove. Paula learned to dot every "i" and cross every "t" and make sure things were documented so they couldn't be spun into something else. She had to "lock down" everything; only then was she safe and was acknowledgment from her father possible.

Paula and Roy's mother was often treated the same way and was pulled into the competition. Be perfect and able to prove it. The people closest to Paula—her brother and her mother—were rivals and adversaries, not allies.

It is significant when a person who prides themselves on being in control loses control. Sometimes the person will try just about anything to avoid acknowledging the loss of control because they perceive themselves to be vulnerable, and they are. However, they perceive vulnerability as weakness, whereas I see vulnerability as strength. When a person comes to understand they cannot truly take control, the truth of the situation finally can come out. The truth is often messy and painful, like pus in a wound, but, to heal, that truth must come out.

I don't believe reexperiencing the past is enough. If that past is relived but the truth is not accepted, where is the healing? You might as well stuff the pus back into the wound and stitch it up again. I believe the past needs to be accepted for what it is—something that cannot be changed in the present. The past cannot be run from (at least not indefinitely); it cannot be wished away or rejected. Instead, I firmly believe the past must be accepted for the truth it represents.

Paula had to accept the adversarial upbringing she experienced. She had to accept that the mother who should have protected her instead considered her a rival. She had to accept that the image of a big brother who looked out for his little sister was false. She had to accept that the father she spent so much energy trying to please was a flawed man whose actions were painful for the entire family.

Start Feeling

Loss produces pain, so using the term "numbing out" is not a coincidence. So many of the survival strategies used by abused children are meant to do just that—provide a way to numb the pain. Paula's relentless pursuit of control was a way to numb out the pain caused by her psychologically abusive childhood. Since she'd devised such an effective (she thought) method to forestall the pain, why in the world would she want to put that aside and actually feel the pain? Why embrace what she'd spent all that time and energy avoiding?

My response to Paula, and to others, is that you may think you're avoiding the pain but you're not. The pain is still there, affecting what you do and how you feel and how you handle your life; you're just pretending it's not. You may think you're not feeling anger at the past, but then why are you negative and hostile with those around you? You may think you're not frustrated or grieving over how you were treated, but why do small setbacks create such large obstacles? Your feelings are there, underneath the numbness and denial, causing pain and creating problems. Bringing your feelings out in the light of day allows you to start seeing them for what they are and how they affect you.

Interrogate Your Feelings

Feeling again is just one step in the healing process. Grief, loss, anger, frustration, and despair are all valid feelings in regard to

123

childhood abuse. People I've worked with sometimes will have an aversion to identifying these feelings accurately, even when they begin to truly feel them without their coping mechanisms.

When I asked Paula if she was angry about her past, at first, she said she was disappointed, as if being treated like that had no more emotional effect on her than learning the grocery store was out of her brand of toothpaste. Of course, she was known to angrily confront store clerks and restaurant servers with extreme displeasure in just that sort of situation. Paula needed to learn that when she said she was disappointed, what she really meant was that she was angry and sad. She also needed to learn that sometimes she got mad about toothpaste because she was mad about her childhood.

When people have devoted themselves to not feeling anything to protect themselves from pain, they can become disconnected from their feelings. Or, if they have chosen a specific feeling to dominate them, they become unused to interacting with all the other emotions humans feel. They become unfamiliar with optimism because they react suspiciously in all situations. They don't remember how to be open because they've spent so much time closing themselves off.

Learning to cry again, to truly belly laugh, to tolerate fear, anger, frustration, or pain without becoming emotionally overwhelmed can be difficult. Some survivors of childhood abuse reintegrate these emotions on their own or with help from family and friends. However, depending on the severity of the abuse, survivors may need the help of a professional counselor or therapist to navigate these waters without finding themselves in over their heads, inundated and gasping for emotional breath. Admitting you need help does not mean you are a failure; rather, admitting you need help and getting the help you need shows the resourcefulness and creativity you used to survive the abuse in the first place.

Accept Your Feelings

"I don't want to feel this way," Paula told me defiantly at one point. "I wouldn't want to, either," I admitted. But feelings are what they are; they are both biochemical and psychological. If you are walking in a field and run across a rattlesnake, chances are you will be startled and feel afraid. Whether you want to be fearful is irrelevant to the fact that you are afraid.

Paula talked about how she felt when her father would voice his displeasure at something she did or didn't do. She would usually first feel a deep sense of shame. Her second response would be to mentally beat herself up. She would feel unworthy and fearful of being vulnerable to collateral attacks from both her brother and her mother. Getting Paula to admit to her feelings wasn't easy. She said talking about them made her feel emotionally naked. I told her there was no shame in being naked; that's how everyone enters the world. Then I asked her to remember the birth of her own children and how she'd held them, naked, in her arms without any sense of shame.

Accepting your feelings doesn't necessarily mean those feelings were good or right or even appropriate. Acceptance means just that—you accept that is how you felt. Once you accept how you felt, you can begin to examine those feelings in greater depth.

Evaluate More than Feelings

Because Paula's feelings were so painful, she kept trying to explain them away, to shrink back from them, to cover them up as if they were something shameful. Feeling ashamed doesn't make you shameful. Feeling unworthy doesn't make you worthless. Feeling afraid doesn't make you unsafe. Reality is not based solely on what you feel.

Understanding what you feel is important, but so is recognizing a situation is more than just what you feel about it. Let's go back to the example of walking in the field and running across a rattlesnake.

You felt afraid, in danger, and you certainly reacted that way. But was that all there was to the situation? What if that rattlesnake was really a gnarled stick that just looked like a rattlesnake? What if that rattlesnake was really a harmless bull snake? Did you feel in danger? Yes. Were you in danger? No. Feelings, being powerful and, often, instantaneous, have the capacity to overshadow other aspects of the situation that you should also be paying attention to.

Because Paula kept deflecting her feelings regarding her past, she also kept herself from really evaluating the circumstances of that past. Growing up, she often felt humiliated, ashamed, and unworthy. Those feelings became set in stone because Paula refused to go back, as an adult, and evaluate those experiences. When her father reprimanded her for some real or imagined indiscretion, had she felt ashamed? Yes. Was she a shameful person? No. When he made her feel unworthy of love, did she feel that way? Yes. Was she an unlovable person? No. When her brother or her mother attacked her as well, did she feel she deserved it? Yes. Did she deserve their attacks? No. Accepting that you felt a certain way is only discovering one component of the truth.

Adopt a Hazy View

As I worked with Paula to reexperience and reevaluate her past, her husband, Will, became an active and integral partner. Paula grew up in a black-and-white world where any hint of grey meant abject failure. Within this either-or worldview, Paula had difficulty connecting to the hazier state of reality. Paula insisted her father had been right for berating her over her failure to place in a high school band competition, but Will gently reminded her she had told him she had spent the week before ill with a terrible flu.

In an ideal world, no one ever gets sick or tired or makes a mistake, but that is not the world we live in. People cannot be 100 percent, 100 percent of the time. To expect such perfection is to assure a sense of failure. Childhood abuse can create rigid either-or thinking, where you are convinced you are always at fault. You're either at fault because you deserved the abuse or you're at fault because you couldn't stop the injustice of the abuse.

Paula grew up so focused on her own imperfections that she forgot her mother, father, and brother were imperfect too. As part of her healing, Paula began to look at her father, her mother, and her brother as imperfect, flawed people. She started to remember times when she was older and her father had verbally attacked her mother. Paula had sat by silently, secretly taking satisfaction in her mother's humiliation, glad she wasn't the target. Paula remembered her brother rarely being in the household as he got older and leaving for the military right out of high school. She had thought he had wanted to get away from her, but now she realized he was just trying to escape the household—something she hadn't been able to do until after college.

Paula was even able to think about her father and how so much in life was disappointing to him. She remembered him angrily denouncing coworkers and bosses for lost opportunities. She remembered how no one ever came to their house to visit and he never went to visit anyone except family, and that happened only rarely. Paula thought her father was disappointed in her but came to realize her father was disappointed in life. The rattlesnake she was so afraid of turned out to be an old, twisted stick of a man, gnarled by his own unhappiness. Paradoxically, by accepting a hazier worldview than the black-and-white one she'd grown up in, Paula's childhood came into clearer view.

Learn to Live in the Present

Paula grew up convinced that life was going to be difficult, that the world was full of rattlesnakes all out to hurt her. What conclusion was she to draw based on what she had experienced growing up? But Paula needed to learn to let go of that conclusion, even though it had promised to keep her safe from being bitten by the world. Sometimes what frightens you is really a gnarled stick or a harmless bull snake and there's no reason to stay afraid and refuse to walk in meadows. Sometimes meadows are full of soft grass and beautiful flowers and well worth the trip.

Survivors of childhood abuse sometimes spend too much time looking over their shoulders, running from the fears of their past. Sometimes they spend too much time peering off into the horizon for signs of future danger. Stuck in either the past or the future or both, they can miss out on the here-and-now, leaving no room to relax and enjoy today.

"Life on life's terms" is a way to relax and live in the moment, whether that moment is happy or sad or indifferent. The past cannot be changed and the future is yet to be experienced. The only thing in play, really, is right now.

Anticipate the Positive

Like Paula, some people keep waiting for the right conditions to happen to be happy but constantly find that the right conditions never come. Paula's impossibly high standard for happiness meant she was constantly unhappy. Unhappy, anxious, suspicious, and agitated, Paula's outer response reflected her inner negativity. She overlooked the content of her daughter's school assignment because she was concerned about the typos in the draft. She neglected to acknowledge the thank-you she received for a current work project because she was worried she would fail the next one. She never saw the smile from the bagger at the grocery store because she was focused on the toothpaste the store didn't have in stock.

I've always heard the phrase "self-fulfilling prophecy," but I didn't realize there was an actual definition. Granted, this is from Wikipedia, but still, I found it interesting: "A self-fulfilling prophecy is a prediction that directly or indirectly causes itself to become true, by the very terms of the prophecy itself, due to positive feedback between belief and behavior."[1] Can positive feedback between belief and behavior happen in negative prophecies? I think so. When you are so sure disasters wait just around the next corner, when you get there, you find one.

The great thing about self-fulfilling prophecies is they can go both ways. Another way to think of this is found in phrases such as "Every dark cloud has a silver lining" or "It's darkest just before dawn." If you believe the sun will come out tomorrow and tomorrow is only a day away, then chances are the sun will come out tomorrow, which is really only a day away. Intentionally looking for the positive ensures you'll find it, which is illustrated by phrases such as "If you think you can or you can't, you're right" or "You always find what you're looking for." The lesson is to be careful what you look for.

Because Paula kept looking for the negative, that's what she found. And because she always found the negative, she kept proving herself right. When she started to adjust her vision to anticipate the positive, she found the world—and the people in it—wasn't as negative as she thought.

Embrace the Positive

Children who have been abused can grow up to be distrustful of anything good happening or anything good lasting. Sometimes the abuser used positives as potential rewards that were short-lived or never materialized. Anything positive, then, becomes something temporary, at best, or a trap, at worst. Growing up this way makes trusting in the positives difficult. Fully embracing something positive can seem fraught with danger. What if it isn't as positive as it seems? What if I'm disappointed again? If something good happens to me, doesn't that mean something bad must happen to even the score?

Paula grew up suspicious of positives and withheld them from her husband and children. She was afraid if she gave them praise, they might stop trying to please her. One difficult exercise I had Will and Paula do when they first started counseling with me was to sit across from each other, hold hands, and tell what they liked and respected about each other. Will was able to handle the exercise well. Paula, however, had difficulty. She would start into a positive but then qualify it. She was stuck on the word *but*.

Healing from childhood abuse means not only recognizing that positives exist but also allowing them to exist without qualification. A child's drawing is beautiful whether the lines were followed or the sky is green. People are capable of kindness even if they're not always kind. A spectacular sunrise in the morning need not be spoiled by rain in the evening. Positive things happen all around us—discreet and distinct. If you allow the negatives that invariably happen to cancel out the positives, the negatives always win.

Reciprocate the Positive

With Paula and Will, I tried that "positive" exercise at the beginning of counseling and again near the end. An enormous breakthrough happened the second time, when Paula could relax and praise her husband without qualification. She also praised aspects of his character, such as patience, kindness, and faithfulness. The first time, Paula had chosen examples of how Will performed tasks, such as keeping the cars running or handling the taxes, as her positives. This time, she embraced Will for who he was instead of what he did.

Letting go of the pain of the past can be quite difficult for survivors of childhood abuse. Without realizing it, they have integrated the pain—acknowledged or not—into their personal identity. They use this identity to focus attention on themselves, to manipulate others to get what they want. Seeing themselves as damaged because of the pain can become a familiar viewpoint, especially when they don't believe they deserve to be viewed any other way.

Until a person can acknowledge the pain and then learn from it and release it, the pain will remain. A person in pain is a self-focused person; pain will do that—just knock your toe into a table leg and you'll be focused, fast. Healing allows a person to let go of the pain and choose a new identity, a new way of interacting with the world that allows for the positive, for self, and for others. When positives become part of a person's world, the natural tendency is to freely share those positives with others, not be fearful of them or attempt to hoard them for yourself.

The Healing Journey

Paula and Will spent time, energy, and resources to cultivate healing in their lives—individually and in their relationship. They spent time not only with me as a couple, but they also spent time with each other and alone, working through their separate issues. They could have devoted that time to other things, as they had earlier in their marriage. Paula could have remained immersed in her work, her home, her kids. Will could have continued to retreat to various hobbies and activities to take a break from Paula's relentless negativity. They could have, but they didn't.

Both Will and Paula contributed energy to their individual and joint healing. Paula's energy may have been more demonstrative than Will's, as she wrestled with past pain and decades worth of inadequate coping strategies. Will added in his own positive energy, as well as his love for Paula, his belief in their relationship, and his commitment to their children.

Finally, they accepted the use of their resources for this purpose. They could have bought material things to make them happy for a while but chose instead to invest in something less tangible, perhaps, but more enduring—each other. Not every "Paula" has a "Will" to go through this healing process with her. But I have found others are willing to walk alongside the hurting person—if not a family member, then a close, trustworthy friend. When that is not possible, healing can still take place, as the person learns to become their own best friend.

What about you? Do you believe you have the capacity to stop running and accept your past? Are you willing to start feeling what you've been avoiding, to learn to interrogate those feelings for truth and accept them for what they are? Can you learn to move past your feelings and evaluate a broader picture? Do you want to become a person able to live in the present, even with a "hazy" view? Can you see yourself coming full circle as a person able to anticipate a positive future, fully embrace that future without fear, and give back to others the gift of your optimism, hope, and joy?

Speaking of hope, I hope you can say yes. Starting fresh and learning new skills is a gift from God, who, James says, generously gives wisdom to all who ask and never finds fault in the request (see James 1:5). Recovery, reconciliation, and renewal are possible. I've seen it in the lives of many people who took the risk and said yes.

9

Steps to Cognitive Healing

"You're an idiot."

"How can you be so stupid?"

"Why can't you be smart like your sister?"

"You're as dumb as your mother."

"You're not college material."

"How did you ever graduate from high school?"

"You'll never amount to anything."

"I'll never amount to anything so why even try?"

If you are told repeatedly that you'll never amount to anything, the danger is you'll believe it and stop trying. Childhood abuse not only damages who a person is, it also sabotages who a person believes they can become.

Cognitive Behavioral Therapy

In my line of work, one of the basic methods used for therapeutic recovery is called cognitive behavioral therapy (CBT). In CBT, a person is counseled on how to develop the skills to change their thoughts (cognitive patterns) so that they can begin to change their behavior. Change the underlying thoughts and change the behavior. At the root of this approach is an assumption that a person can understand their thoughts well enough to make the necessary changes.

But what if you were told from the time you were a child that you weren't smart, that you didn't have the capacity to understand anything complex? What if others demonstrated by their actions that trying to change your situation or circumstances was useless or even caused things to get worse? What if you stopped believing in anything changing because of the pain you felt when disappointed?

The word *cognition* means the mental process of acquiring knowledge and understanding through thought, experience, and the senses. But what if your childhood abuse created a thought process riddled with doubt, anxiety, frustration, and fear? What if, because of childhood abuse, your experiences growing up were predominantly negative? And what if you learned not to trust your senses because of the trauma you suffered? Is it any wonder that a survivor of childhood abuse would need to reach for new ways of thinking to promote healing?

What if neglect was part of your early childhood experience? What if you were routinely denied adequate food or sleep? What if books and games were nonexistent for you growing up except in school? What if you were left alone with a television screen, at most? What if you were starved physically, emotionally, or intellectually? Abuse takes a toll on the body and the mind. Researchers have only lately begun to study the detrimental cognitive effects of what has been termed ELS (early life stress).[1]

Cognitive Dissonance

Cognitive healing takes an intentional strategy to realign cognitive distortions created through childhood abuse. Remember, cognition happens through thought, experiences, and senses. These three elements of cognition can become hijacked by childhood abuse and must be realigned with reality. The bedrock of cognition is thought, so what you think becomes vitally important.

In therapy, there is a concept known as "cognitive dissonance." This is an anxiety condition that results when a person tries to hold on to two incompatible thoughts at the same time. For example, a person who grew up with childhood abuse may have a strong belief that people are untrustworthy. However, when that person is around people who are genuinely trustworthy, the evidence does not match the belief, creating dissonance. This dissonance, in turn, leads to discomfort. Instead of jettisoning the false belief that people are untrustworthy, the person, instead, may abandon the trustworthy people and seek out untrustworthy individuals who match the belief.

One challenge of recovery from childhood abuse lies in this cognitive dissonance between what an abused child comes to believe as true and the truth of the broader world. I believe cognitive healing happens when a person changes and modifies those beliefs derived from unhealthy, abusive pasts and realize harmony through present-day experiences and updated beliefs.

You are not stupid. Over the years, I've been surprised by how many successful people carry this destructive seed of doubt about their own intellectual abilities. They were told they were stupid or treated as stupid growing up, and even though they may have fought virulently against this perception into adulthood, they are still terrified this falsehood is true. For these individuals, any success is an aberration, a circumstantial house of cards just waiting to tumble down around them. In a perverse way, if disaster strikes, they experience a sense of relief as circumstances are brought back into alignment with the false belief. But this sense of relief is a trap, a prison of low expectations and assured failure. A person must believe in their ability to intellectually grasp new information and concepts, to accept new and positive viewpoints.

You are not in danger. A person who has survived childhood abuse is, literally, hardwired to expect danger. They have been conditioned to react instinctively to avoid, attempt to avoid, or survive pain. Dangerous situations come with their own rules, which are generally no rules beyond finding a way to escape and survive. Dangerous situations produce a sort of tunnel vision that requires them to filter out extraneous, outside details to focus on the immediate circumstances. A propensity for intense tunnel vision can make it difficult for a person to expand their perception to take in the viewpoints of other people, including long-term consequences of present actions. Seeing yourself as being in danger when you are not artificially narrows your responsive options to people and situations. You may tend to react negatively instead of responding positively. When you feel safe, you open up and so does your world.

You are not worthless. People do not, generally, put forth great effort for items of little or no value. If you believe you are an item of little or no value, you may not put in much effort on your own behalf. You may presuppose that others will not put out much effort on your behalf, either. You may settle for the crumbs that come your way instead of going out and creating a meal for yourself. When you feel you have worth, you expect worthwhile things in response from yourself and others.

You are not unlovable. People love things they value. If you believe you have no value, then you are sure no one could or should love you. And you, certainly, can find no love for yourself. By considering yourself unlovable, you remove yourself from contention for the attention, affection, and effort of others. If your childhood experiences reflect the negative attention, affection, and effort of others, you may choose to stay invisible to feel safe. But love is an essential part of the human experience. You may not have experienced love growing up, but you shouldn't throw away the potential for love going forward.

You are not doomed to fail. Ever heard sayings such as "No pain, no gain" or "No risk, no reward"? If you are convinced pain will not produce gain and risk will not produce reward, then why should you undergo pain and risk for nothing? If failure is assured, then why not at least settle for some assurance in an identity of failure? To effect change, you must move from where you are to someplace different. And to find the motivation to move, you must believe you can move and that you are moving to a better place. If you don't, you'll stay stuck where you are and failure will remain a false place of safety.

You are not destined to stay a victim. Childhood abuse incubates feelings of powerlessness. You may begin to view yourself as constantly fighting against forces stronger than you, determined to bring you down, to teach you a lesson, to put you in your place. These forces may have begun with distinct faces and direct actions of harm, but they eventually morphed into faceless influences orchestrating indirect actions of harm. You come to believe others are against you, the world is against you, God is against you, life is against you. How can you expect yourself to overcome such big and powerful forces? The most you determine you can do is to somehow survive, just like you did as a child. To recover you must determine that survival is not enough.

The above examples are, by no means, a complete compilation of the negative thoughts that can burrow into a person's mind-set through childhood abuse. Instead, they are meant as an illustration of how cognition can be impaired through faulty and false beliefs. To effect change and healing, you must learn to interrogate and reject your thoughts and beliefs, even those you are convinced kept you safe, or at least safer, throughout your childhood and still have value today. Each thought and belief needs to be able to stand on its own, within a healthy, positive mind-set and worldview.

The knowledge and understanding of cognition happens not only through what you think but also through what you experience. What you *know* and what you *understand* can become warped by the experiences of childhood abuse. Once you can begin to discard faulty beliefs, you may find you open up new avenues to interpret the experiences you have. As I said before, childhood abuse can create a sort of tunnel vision, with you and your safety at the nexus point. But not everything that happens to you is because of you. A person who cuts you off on the freeway may be texting and oblivious to your need to get to work. A computer that crashes is not exhibiting electronic retaliation against you personally. A coworker who gets sick right before you're supposed to leave for vacation has a virus, not a vendetta. When you are able to free yourself from faulty and false beliefs about yourself and others, you're better able to cognitively engage in discovering the truth about yourself, others, and specific circumstances.

The third leg of cognition is the senses. However, a person in a state of anxiety, stress, or depression operates under impairment. A stressed or anxious person has hypervigilant senses that may perceive danger when none is present. A stressed or numbed out person has dulled senses, which weaken their ability to sense the positive.

Cognitive Distractions

Chad came to me because he had been diagnosed with ADD as an adult. As a child, he'd struggled in school and had spent more time in detention than he could remember. He wanted help to, as he put it, "conquer" this diagnosis without medications. He didn't want pills; he wanted procedures, skills he could use to help deal with his admitted distractibility.

Chad freely acknowledged he'd always had trouble paying attention in school, that he seemed to bounce around from activity to activity, never settling on any one thing for long. He confessed to being somewhat impulsive and said that tendency had gotten him into trouble a time or two growing up. Chad also outlined other symptoms, such as difficulty concentrating and staying organized. His life, he said, always seemed chaotic, which had been somewhat exciting as a teenager, but now, as an adult, was becoming plain exhausting.

As we talked about his life and how these symptoms were impacting him, I noticed Chad would periodically throw in negative comments about himself and his performance. As I dug deeper, he gave details that indicated his job instability was partially due to a persistent fear that he'd "wear out his welcome," that the more people got to know him, the less they would like or think of him. His impulsivity turned out to be more about finding a lavish way to finally prove himself. Rather than thrill-seeking, I perceived he was worth-seeking. The more Chad talked, the more convinced I became that at least some of his ADD symptoms stemmed from the psychological and physical abuse he, eventually, could admit he had suffered.

Because of the abuse, so much of Chad's life was spent on the run and under stress, making himself a moving target. Belittled and humiliated, he was terrified of failure and chose staged, grandiose schemes for recognition over methodical, day-to-day efforts that, in his childhood experience, were rarely acknowledged. His ruminating, negative beliefs from childhood so consumed his inner thought life that he had little room left in adulthood to remember things such as renewing his license or paying his property taxes or picking up his child from school.

Chad had stated he didn't want to go on medication, and I left that decision between him and his doctor. Our work together was twofold. The first was changing his underlying faulty beliefs so he could counter his negative thoughts, realign his experiences, and unlock his senses to what was happening to him today. The second was helping him develop behaviors that would support greater remembrance and organization. We started with the second to help with the first. Together, we agreed to the following strategies:

- *Keep a master list.* When I suggested Chad keep a task list so he wouldn't forget things, he said he'd already tried that. In fact, he said, he had more lists than he could keep up with and he kept misplacing them. I suggested Chad use his phone as his "portable brain." We worked on setting up his calendar as a way to remember tasks or events, including scheduling alerts that could be changed from a week out to an hour out as the task or event got closer.

- *Do it now.* Since Chad could be so forgetful, I suggested he immediately do any task he was able to do, such as sorting through the mail after work. We discovered that Chad was a notorious procrastinator because he constantly fretted that he wouldn't do the task correctly or that now wasn't the best time and it was better to put things off when he could "think about it." We identified this as a fear reaction of inadequacy.

- *Plan for time.* Chad was constantly late. He would get caught up in unimportant things and be late for or forget the important ones. Again, using his phone, we worked out a way for Chad to set a timer, in addition to calendar alerts, to provide a time structure for the tasks he needed to do. Chad was incredibly frustrated with this method until we discovered he was giving himself too little time to get things done. He consistently thought he should be able to do things faster and was distressed by how long tasks actually took him. Again, this uncovered a fear reaction because, growing up, Chad was derided or even beaten if he did not accomplish tasks within an unrealistic time frame. Quick came to mean safer.

- *Plan ahead.* Because Chad distrusted his ability to succeed, he often would delay thinking about future events. Thinking about them produced anxiety, so he simply didn't. Instead, he tended to, as he put it, "wing it" and make do last minute. I suggested that some of his anxiety might lessen if he took the time to plan out what he would need and when, even down to setting out the night before what he wanted to wear for an important event or meeting. That way, if he'd forgotten to wash that favorite shirt or his shoes needed polishing, he would have the time to deal with those details. I suggested being able to know beforehand that he had what he needed should reduce the anxiety he felt about failing at the event.

- *First things first.* One of the hardest strategies for Chad was to stick with doing one thing at a time. He would start a task and then, in the middle of doing that task, become distracted by three or four other things, meaning he didn't get any of them done. His avoidance of completing a task, we learned, came from his discipline growing up. Chad never knew what he would be punished for, from something significant to something so trivial that he didn't even notice it. And his punishments were equally harsh, whether the task was big or small. To help Chad stay on chore, we devised a basket system at his home and work where he could place discreet tasks, such as paying bills, in a single basket instead of having a huge, distracting pile of mail to sort through.

When Chad forgot things, he felt like a failure. When he failed, he felt stupid. When he felt stupid, he felt worthless. When he felt worthless, he became depressed. When he became depressed, he lost concentration and forgot things.

As Chad spent less time ruminating about the past, he had more time to act in the present and plan for the future. As he felt himself gain a greater sense of accomplishment and progress, his anxiety, stress, and fear subsided, freeing up more time and energy for positive thoughts and experiences. As Chad's life became a healthier mix of positive and negative, he could view the world without the restricting negative-only blinders of the past.

Researchers may, finally, be quantifying the cognitive damage done through childhood abuse in general, but my focus will remain on the healing and recovery that can happen one person at a time. Was Chad damaged by the abuse he suffered? Yes, but he found a way to compensate and heal. I have found great resilience in survivors of childhood abuse, even those scarred by the worst abuse and neglect. They have shed themselves of any responsibility for the abuse, yet they have repeatedly taken up the mantle of accountability for finding ways to overcome and work around obstacles in their paths. Their abusers tried to make them less, yet they are determined to create ways to become more. This quality is the heart of perseverance, a quality I have found prevalent in so many people who have survived childhood abuse.

10

Steps to Physical Healing

Kendra lived her life as a bundle of stress. She was anxious about everything. Her job. Her family. Her health. The older she got, the more she worried that the time, energy, and effort she'd put into each of these areas of her life was going to backfire and she'd end up washed up, rejected, and sick. Kendra was so consumed with worry that she finally had to take a leave of absence from work. Her family was worn out trying to handle her anxieties and their requirements. Kendra developed high blood pressure and panic attacks.

As long as Kendra could remember, she felt at war with her body. When she was younger, she just wanted to be older and beyond things like acne and puberty. When she was older, she kept trying to force her body to be younger through a series of yo-yo diets and late-night herbal miracles. Kendra continually felt betrayed by a body that tired out just when she needed it to do more. She learned she just couldn't trust it. So, Kendra began to obsessively monitor her body—what it was doing, how she was feeling—waiting for something to go wrong. Kendra had learned early on that things always went wrong.

Hypervigilance can be a by-product of childhood abuse. Even the thought of relaxing, of letting down one's guard, produces stress, fear, and anxiety. When you feel you're never safe, your body is under siege. Over years, this takes a physical toll, as I talked about earlier. To encourage recovery from childhood abuse, you must begin to view your body as a precious gift, something to be grateful for and worthy of protection.

Matthew never gave much thought to his body—precious or not. His body was supposed to obey his orders. For many years, it complied. He figured an hour in the gym twice a week bought him the right to ask of his body whatever he wanted. When his body was too tired, he drank caffeine, lots of it. When his body was too strung out, he popped nighttime sleep aids. His body was not supposed to show any weakness. Weakness, Matthew thought, was dangerous and unacceptable. His body was supposed to allow him to keep fulfilling his plans, as it always had.

And then, it didn't. Matthew was at a loss as to what to do. All his life, he'd known the only person he could really rely on was himself. Then he became physically unreliable. Matthew was devastated at this display of weakness. The foundation he'd built his life around—his ability to perform—crumbled, as Matthew's life became a series of hospital visits and doctors telling him what to do. He became depressed, which is how I came to work with him.

Both Kendra and Matthew spent years, decades really, neglecting their physical health. When they were younger, they took that health for granted. When they got older, they shoved that health onto a back burner of priorities because they were consumed with the demands of their anxiety, stress, and negativity.

Both had developed faulty beliefs about their health. Kendra assumed she could take a pill or an herb or a powder and make everything work perfectly. Matthew assumed everything would always work, no matter what he did. Both were wrong.

Recovery from childhood abuse requires healing on a variety of levels. One level that tends to be overlooked is the physical level. Once the scars, bruising, and welts heal, people often falsely assume the physical consequences are over. But just as emotional and cognitive healing requires intentionality and effort, so does physical healing. Fortunately, the body has a great capacity for recovery and restoration.

The body is neither an enemy, as Kendra believed, nor a silent partner, as Matthew believed. Both refused to listen to their bodies and, instead, did all the talking. Or, rather, their inner negativity did all the talking. Many of the clients I have worked with have ignored their bodies' needs in a myriad of ways—from starving to bingeing, from substance abuse to supplement abuse, from those who never stop to rest to those who never rise to move.

The body is a complex system of muscles and tendons, neurotransmitters and hormones, of systems you see and systems you don't. In contrast to the complexity of the human body is the simplicity of physical restoration. Though I'm not a medical professional, I've found a short list of interventions that can help the body to recover. I've been recommending the first five for years.

Healthy Eating

This first recommendation sounds so simple—eat healthy—yet I've found people have a difficult time accomplishing this. People at my clinic work with me as well as with registered dietitians who are trained to understand the connection between what you eat and how you feel. While the dietitians' interaction with each person is individualized, they teach certain constants:

- Eat whole foods. These include fresh fruits, vegetables, and whole-grain products. Our dietitians teach people to shop the "outside" of the grocery store, where the produce, dairy, and meats are found, and to avoid the inner aisles, where many highly processed products are found.

- Avoid artificial anything, from additives to flavorings to sweeteners.
- Don't be afraid of healthy fats and oils, especially flaxseed and olive and canola oil.
- Watch for hidden added sugars, trans fats, and salts.
- Round out your meals with a mix of healthy carbohydrates, fats, and proteins.

Healthy eating is not only what you eat, but how you eat. Have you ever found yourself cramming down food in the heat of the moment, only to finish and have no real recollection of what you just ate? Food is not a necessary evil nor is a meal meant to be an indulgent free-for-all. Food should be consumed intentionally, with awareness of what you are eating. A meal is not a race to the finish line, either. So often our dietitians must help people learn to slow down when they eat, to savor flavors and textures, to chew and not just consume.

Survivors of childhood abuse can have difficulty eating healthy. Sometimes they were not taught what a healthy meal looks like. Other times they grew up scavenging for themselves, the only criteria for a meal being what tasted the best. Sometimes the abuse they suffered involved food—food was withheld through neglect or punishment or used as way to force compliance. Mealtimes may have been battle zones to be avoided at all costs. Food may have become the only reliable pleasure in a chaotic world. Or food may have been the one way to exhibit some level of control.

Depending on how food and meals factored into your abusive childhood, eating healthy may be compromised. You may not know what healthy eating looks like or feels like. If food, and your relationship to food, has become tangled up with your childhood abuse, please don't despair. Mental health and medical professionals can work in tandem to help you unlock what's not working and teach you what will.

Exercise

I tend to use the word *exercise* for this recommendation because, if I said "movement," some of you might get the wrong idea. But these words really could be used interchangeably. You don't have to become a gym rat to be healthy. Rather, you need to find ways, both structured and casual, to move more. We don't move enough; at least, I know I wouldn't unless I was intentional about it. I sit at a desk. I sit at a computer. I sit in a chair. I sit in my car. I sit on my couch. Because I sit so much, I need to find ways to move more. And because I'm busy, I need to assign importance and priority to getting out and moving. Otherwise, an entire day has gone by and all I've done is sit.

Some people get plenty of one kind of exercise on their jobs (mail carriers come to mind), but the body is made up of more than legs or arms. The whole body should be moved and stretched, extended and pushed. Of course, the goal is to benefit the body, not to push the body too far. Knowing the difference can be confusing, so I always recommend people work with their physicians or a personal trainer (the personal trainer at my clinic also happens to be a registered nurse) to ease into exercise if they are new to it or ease up on exercise if they're overdoing it.

Hydration

I've heard varying percentages over the years about the adequate amount of water humans should consume per day, but what stays consistent is that many Americans walk around every day chronically dehydrated. In short, we don't drink enough water. Notice, I didn't say liquid. We drink plenty of soda and coffee and other beverages, but not enough water. Sodas and coffee often contain caffeine, which is a natural diuretic. A diuretic is anything that causes you to urinate more frequently.

You know you need to drink more water, but how much is enough? The answer depends on your gender, body size, geographic location, and how much you sweat. The "right" amount of water for you might vary from day to day, depending on where you are and what you're doing. Since many of us are unintentionally dehydrated, it makes sense that we would need to become more intentional about the water we drink.

Proper hydration involves not only avoiding too little water but also avoiding too much. Too much water leaches important components from your body and can create health issues. There is a way to determine if you're drinking enough and that's to, somewhat crudely, apply the pee test. If your urine is dark, you need to drink more water. The goal is pale or clear.

When you're dehydrated, your body starts sending you signals. However, these signals can be misinterpreted. Instead of reaching for something to drink, you may reach for something to eat because the body can extract water from foods. If you have a headache or feel weak, you may think you're hungry, when you're really dehydrated.

From what I've read, the human body is 60 percent water. Water is the lubricant for our muscles and our brains. We need water to digest food, absorb vitamins and minerals, and flush out our kidneys. A hydrated body contributes to a healthy body.

Sleep Hygiene

When is the last time you had a restful night's sleep? I hope you're able to say "last night." Unfortunately, in my line of work, I often hear people say, "I can't really remember." Anxiety, depression, and stress all interfere with the body's ability to reach a state of healthy sleep and to stay there. Some people I work with dread nighttime because they know sleep will be a battle.

Those who have suffered childhood abuse can have a difficult time achieving restful sleep. For some, the abuse they experienced may have occurred in or around the bedroom or at night. Nighttime, then, is not seen as a time to unwind and relax, but a time of increased danger and vigilance. For others, the quiet of night is invaded by the remembered sounds, sights, and smells of their abuse. Nighttime is not a time to relax, but a time to relive. Still others may find it difficult to reach a point of relaxation when their entire day has been spent in frantic activity. Nighttime is not a time to put today to bed, but a time to prep for battle tomorrow.

Whenever it seems necessary, those who come in for treatment at my clinic undergo a sleep study. This sleep study involves wearing a small probe on one finger while you sleep. The probe is attached to a wristband device, which is able to detect sleep/wake cycles and important information such as oxygen levels. A report is generated from the information to give a clear picture of the quality of a person's sleep during that night. This information can then be discussed in length with the person's primary care physician.

Pharmaceutical options are certainly available to help with sleep, but, personally, I believe these should be used only in a limited number of cases. Ideally, the goal is to assist the person in changing attitudes and behaviors that will allow for more restful sleep. Some of these strategies are extremely simple.

- Transition to sleep. Some fortunate people are able to go from fully awake to fully asleep in a matter of minutes. I have never been one of them. Instead, I find it helpful to prepare myself to sleep. I turn off all electronics. I might listen to soft, soothing music or use a dim light to read a relaxing book (no murder mysteries or action novels for me).

- Give yourself enough time. Some days I know I'm going to be short on sleep because of work activities, family commitments, or travel requirements. However, I work to make this the exception and not the rule. Per the National Sleep Foundation, the optimum amount of sleep per night is seven to nine hours. I guess that's where we get the usual eight-hour recommendation.[1]

- Establish a routine. As much as possible, I try to go to bed at the same time each night so I can, hopefully, wake up at the same time each morning. This consistency helps my body develop a rhythm.

- Cut out the caffeine. I live in Seattle; what can I say? I like coffee, but coffee doesn't like my sleep after about three in the afternoon. This doesn't always work, but I really try to avoid caffeine into the evening so I'm not asking my body to wind down at the same time I'm revving it up.

- Snacks only. When I was younger, I used to be able to eat a large amount of pizza and soon after drop into a deep sleep—not anymore. Whenever possible, I avoid eating large amounts of food later in the evening. A small snack is fine, but no more pizza by the slice late into the night.

Some people are resistant to adopting these sleep recommendations. Instead, they want a pill because they believe that as the easier solution. But a drugged sleep is not a healthy sleep. Using prescribed pills or over-the-counter medications or alcohol or illicit drugs is not a healthy or sustainable long-term solution. Not only will natural sleep continue to remain elusive, but there can be very real, detrimental effects from these so-called remedies.

Supplementation

I remember when one young woman arrived for her first day of treatment at my clinic. She had an entire shopping bag loaded with, what seemed like, every nutritional supplement made. The volume of tablets and capsules and powders she consumed daily was staggering. Equally staggering was how ineffective this cornucopia of supplements was. She was taking too many and too much, without a real understanding of what she was consuming and how all of them worked together. I learned that these pills weren't supplementation, in the traditional sense. She wasn't supplementing her food—she wasn't eating much food, just taking supplements.

This example is not what I mean when I say supplementation. Our bodies were designed to receive the bulk of our nutrition from the foods we eat. Realistically, however, most of us need a small amount of supplementation. In most every instance, medical professionals will recommend that people take a high-quality, well absorbed (also called bioavailability) multivitamin and mineral formula. In addition, those of us in the rainy northern climates often need to take additional vitamin D. Our physicians also routinely recommend coenzyme Q-10 and quality fish oil high in omega 3s.

Every person, of course, is different and will have different supplementation needs. Some people come to us chronically depleted and need a wider range of supplements in higher doses. Others are taking medications that interfere with the absorption and utilization of certain vitamins. In addition, stress and alcohol deplete nutrients. Tests can be performed to measure a person's vitamin and mineral levels. Once you know where you are deficient, you can work with a nutritional professional to bring those levels up to optimum.

These nutrients are not "extras." They are the delivery systems the body needs to carry on vital functions. By replenishing what is missing, the body—which includes the brain—can regain normal and healthy functioning.

Healthy eating, exercise, hydration, good sleep hygiene, and supplementation have always been my basic five healthy tips because paying special attention to them has been extremely effective over my thirty-plus years in therapeutic situations. Two others I propose may seem redundant, given previous comments, but I'd like to highlight them further.

Stress Reduction

Stress is like a hole at the bottom of your bucket. The more stress in your life, the more holes you have. The more stress you have, the more you need to keep filling up your bucket to make up for what's being lost. The sad truth is we have more control over the stress in our lives than we think; we punch out too many of our own holes.

Those with backgrounds of childhood abuse, sadly, often become quite familiar and even comfortable with stress. This is the way they grew up, so stress doesn't seem odd or strange. On the contrary, peace and tranquility can seem unnatural and disconcerting. High alert seems safe; relaxation seems dangerous. But the opposite is true. Stress is dangerous and has been called the silent killer.

Standing down from your vigilance can seem like standing up naked—exposed and vulnerable. But stress wars against the five other recommendations I've made. In my experience, stress eating is not healthy eating. Stress wears you out so you have little energy for healthy exercise. Stress sends you reaching for caffeine and sugar instead of pure water. Stress robs you of sleep. Stress depletes nutrients and overpowers supplementation.

A commitment to becoming healthier should not be seen as an avenue to try to accomplish more. A commitment to becoming healthier should be seen as a goal unto itself, one that doesn't need to be justified or rationalized or leveraged with higher productivity and added stress. You deserve to be healthier. You alone are worth it—not what you do but who you are.

Medication Moderation

People don't often come in to see me with shopping bags full of supplements. More commonly, I see people come in with fistfuls of prescription bottles. They enter treatment with a goal to "get off so many meds." In most cases, I agree.

A couple years ago, the Mayo Clinic did a study that found that almost 70 percent of Americans took at least one prescription drug. More than 50 percent took two, and 20 percent were on five or more prescriptions.[2] Prescription medication is not my scope of practice, but the physicians I've worked with have a simple formula for medications—the smallest possible dose for the shortest amount of time for the maximum achievable effect.

Today's pharmaceuticals can be highly effective, but they can also come with negative and, sometimes, dangerous side effects. An adverse drug reaction is always possible, and different drugs can negatively interact with one another. In my experience, a pill may provide an answer, but it may not be the only answer or even the right answer long term.

Hurting people can be desperate people. Desperate people can sometimes reach for an answer that appears to be easy and quick. In all honesty, therapy is, generally, neither. However, when therapy is combined with nutritional and medical interventions, the body and the mind can be brought together to complement and support each other.

11

Steps to Healing Relationships

After his second marriage ended in a nasty divorce, Doug came to counseling for depression. He felt like an utter failure, or, rather, he felt his divorce confirmed what he knew about himself all along—he was an utter failure. Doug had lived through his parents' divorce as a young child and was devastated he was walking down the same path with, now, two failed marriages.

At the beginning of any counseling relationship (and, believe me, counseling is a relationship), I always ask the person to explain their goals for the counseling. What do they want to accomplish through our time together? What changes do they want to make? How do they see their lives becoming better because of our partnership? Doug's goal was to be able to stay in his next marriage. I came to understand early in counseling that Doug was actively looking for love again and was hopeful I could help him be more successful in his next courtship.

Therefore, Doug was not thrilled when I counseled him to put dating on hold for a while. I thought it most important for Doug to concentrate not on his relationship with someone else but on his relationship with himself. I told him, "You don't really like who you are and you don't think very highly of yourself. So why should anyone else?"

Note to Self

Resilient as children are, childhood abuse, in its various forms, can decimate a child's sense of self:

- How would you feel about yourself if you grew up under the weight of unrealistic expectations from others?
- Would you get used to being a target for anger, rage, and hostility and think you deserved it? Or would you lash out at any hint of a repeat of such injustice?
- If you were constantly told you were to blame for what was wrong in the world, would you come to believe it?
- Would the humiliations you suffered cause you to think less of yourself?
- If your thoughts, actions, and opinions were always marginalized, would you assume you had nothing of value to contribute?
- Would you harbor a deep sense of inferiority if you were the least loved in your family and everyone knew it?
- If you grew up as an invisible child whose presence created no wake whatsoever in the flow of the family, would you be content to stay in the background or would you rebel and constantly try to push forward?
- Would you have deep doubts about your ability to navigate life as an adult if you were treated like a baby growing up?
- If you spent vast amounts of time alone, isolated from peers or activities, would other people and social situations make you feel uncomfortable, unequipped, and nervous?

- Would you develop a sense of suspicion and unfamiliarity with affection if affection was routinely withheld from you or used to groom you for sexual exploitation?
- If you were routinely yelled at, sworn at, insulted, and mocked, what would you learn about how one person speaks to another?
- Would you have a distrust of what other people told you if you grew up being lied to?
- If you grew up in a world where you were made to feel unsafe, threatened, and afraid, how easy would it be for you to relax as an adult?
- Would you trust the promises other people make if your experience growing up was that promises were spoken of but never delivered on?
- How would you think about others if the important people in your childhood sexually exploited you or physically harmed you or neglected your needs?

Doug told me he grew up feeling like a tennis ball. When I asked him to explain that statement, he said he was the thing his parents whacked back and forth before, during, and after their divorce to try to score points on each other. About the only topic Doug remembered his parents agreeing on was how disappointed they were with him. He got the distinct impression that each would have been happy to give him to the other one, but neither wanted him full time.

Childhood abuse has the very real capacity to damage a person's sense of self. A damaged sense of self creates complications in a person's relationships with others. I told Doug I thought we needed to work on his relationship with himself first before he would be ready to begin a relationship with anyone else. The next person or the next relationship or the next marriage was not going to "save" Doug. He first had to realize he wasn't in danger by being himself.

A Better Blueprint

In many ways, childhood abuse gives you the blueprint for what not to do in relationships. The difficulty is recognizing the blueprint is faulty when it has become so foundational to your psychic structure growing up. How are you to know where the blueprint is faulty if that's the only blueprint you know? The answer, to me, is to study a different blueprint—a healthier one. Then, as you come to understand the strengths and advantages to the new, healthier blueprint, you can begin to substitute in parts from it to your natural one. Remember, you are not set in stone. You are a work in progress and change is possible.

- *Learn to be realistic about who you are.* In my experience, childhood abuse can create two opposite extremes. On the one side, some who have been abused as children internalize their abuse and blame themselves. They take responsibility for every bad thing that happens to them. On the other side, some are so full of rage about the injustice they suffered, they refuse to accept any responsibility at all for the choices they make. On the one side, they are responsible for everything. On the other side, they are responsible for nothing. Neither extreme is true.
- *Learn to forgive yourself.* Forgiveness is an amazingly powerful tool for creating and maintaining healthy relationships. (I'll talk more about the power of forgiveness in the final chapter on spiritual healing.) Forgiving yourself is an act of love and, as a survivor of childhood abuse, you may find it difficult. If you believe you are unlovable, this will be difficult. If you are fueled by anger and rage, this will be difficult. People can and do mess up, including you.
- *Be your own best advocate.* An advocate is someone who lends support to another. In your case, learn how to best

advocate for yourself. Discounting your own needs by constantly giving in to others does not support you in the long run. Overstating your own needs by being pushy, loud, demanding, or angry does not support you in the long run. You become your own best advocate when you learn how to present your needs appropriately for support. You also support yourself by finding people who are willing and able to provide that support.

- *Be honest and gentle with yourself.* You'll notice I added gentle to the characteristic of honesty. There is such a thing as being brutally honest. Brutal truth hurts; gentle truth heals. I don't know about you, but I know for myself I am much more willing to accept a difficult truth when that truth is delivered with gentleness. I have a much easier time grasping that truth if it isn't white-hot with anger, rage, or condemnation.

- *Remember the positive.* I believe there is such a thing as a negative mind set. I'm sure you know people who can look at just about any situation and see the negative. The negative says, for example, that soft and cuddly puppy so quick to lick your nose will only grow up to bite your leg. When that happens, you let go of the puppy. Stop. Don't let go of the puppy! Learn to enjoy life's positive, beautiful, and uplifting moments for the gifts they are. Putting down the puppy isn't prudent; it's sad, especially when the puppy is someone you love.

The Blueprint of a Healthy Communicator

Over the years, I've learned how important both verbal and nonverbal communication is in a relationship. Healthy communication, then, requires a new blueprint for those who have experienced childhood abuse. Since the early days of my counseling practice,

I have educated clients on my Twelve Steps to Healthy Communication, which I use to help people learn to recognize and avoid faulty communication patterns in relationships:

1. *Approach your interactions with yourself and others with an attitude of openness and gentleness.* Whether you are dealing with only yourself or with other people, first, beware of the danger of negative patterns of hostility, sarcasm, cynicism, or criticism. These poison your interactions before they've even begun. Second, avoid being overly deferential or simply telling people what they (or you) want to hear. The first is not gentle and the second is not open.

2. *Don't immediately assume you're right.* Having an opinion is fine, but so is holding that opinion until you've had a chance to hear different sides of the issue. This applies to handling conflict with as well as talking to yourself. For example, don't assume you're right if you believe you're worthless. How you feel about an issue or situation should absolutely be factored in, but please be aware that other information needs to be included for you to come to a right conclusion.

3. *Speak the truth to help, not harm.* We talked about this before, but healthy communication requires truth-telling. Yet the truth needs to be presented as a pathway to deeper understanding. Helping truth opens that door; harmful truth too often slams shut the door to understanding.

4. *Concentrate on what to say more than how you feel.* This was one of Doug's biggest barriers in relationships. What he was saying often got drowned out by the emotional intensity he felt while saying it. His intensity frightened and alienated the very people he most wanted to understand what he was saying. Doug grew up without a model of how to handle and filter his thoughts. Through his parents, he learned a pattern

of verbally venting intense negative thoughts and emotions, without considering the effect it had on others. I suggested to Doug that when he felt himself becoming overwhelmed by his emotions, it was not the time to share his thoughts. Instead, I encouraged him to spend time writing down his thoughts. Later, he could read through them and decide how best to present them.

5. *Be aware of different perspectives.* What is obvious to you may not be obvious to someone else. Life experience, cultural markers, age, and gender all play a role in a person's perspective. Go slow; take your time to explain or clarify. Neither of you are at fault or incompetent; you just don't understand each other yet. Be patient and you will.

6. *Be aware of different opinions.* People of different perspectives can come to the same conclusion, but not always. Childhood abuse, especially psychological abuse, can make tolerating different opinions challenging. In the face of different opinions, some people will automatically capitulate, discounting their own opinion as less important than another. Other people will automatically attack, vigorously defending their own opinion as more important than the other. Differences of opinion need not create an "us or them" scenario. Healthy communication allows for the possibility of agreeing to disagree.

7. *Take control of your part in the conversation.* You cannot control the other person, no matter how hard you try. However, you can influence them. One way you can influence the other person is by how you choose to communicate. Model a healthy, positive presentation, and perhaps you will influence the other person to at least try to do the same.

8. *Interrogate your motivation.* At times in my life I have started a conversation with my wife or one of my boys when I've

been decidedly out of sorts. Part of me warned myself not to start, but another part of me was looking to vent some of my feelings of frustration or discomfort, which had nothing to do with whom I was talking to. My family members were convenient, and sadly, I used them. A background of childhood abuse can create a well of frustration and discomfort, along with other negative emotions, that you may be tempted to vent onto others.

9. *Acknowledge the control of the other person.* This may seem counterintuitive when looking through the lens of childhood abuse, but allow me to explain what I mean here. When you are dealing with another person, the only person you have control over is you. You cannot make the other person love you more or treat you better or give you what you need. People control their own decisions. By giving people control over their decisions, you also give them the responsibility for their decisions. If they don't love you more or treat you better or give you what you want, you are not responsible.

10. *Seek to understand the other person.* Doug came to recognize this was an area that damaged his relationship with his first wife. They were both young, and Doug was fresh from living under the abusive influences of his parents. The hurt was raw, and Doug spent much of those early years of that marriage focusing on his own pain and frustration. His first wife, who had wounds and needs of her own, felt neglected and, before long, found someone else willing to listen to and empathize with her. Healthy communication involves two-way communication, which isn't about word count as much as how each person's words count with the other.

11. *Admit when you're wrong.* Again, childhood abuse can produce a pattern of polar extremes. Don't admit to being wrong when you're not. Abusive messages in childhood can

cause you to assume blame when no blame is warranted, so you'll need to be aware of that trap. However, some people have an aversion to accepting any blame because the punishments meted out in childhood were excessive. They learned to admit nothing for fear of intense retaliation. In healthy relationships, admitting you're wrong allows the other person to forgive and move on, which means you can as well.

12. *Do what you say.* Being accountable for what you say allows you to live honestly with yourself and others. Those who grew up doubting their ability may say they will do something, only to have fear derail any efforts to follow through. Those who grew up with a pattern of lying and broken promises may have picked up the habit. My advice is not to promise lightly, and always follow through.

Managing Conflict

For the survivor of childhood abuse, conflict can be a difficult situation. Conflict puts the needs or wants of one person in contention with the needs or wants of another. Because we are different people, with different needs and wants, conflict is inevitable. The question, then, becomes not how to avoid conflict, which is unavoidable, but how to manage conflict. The key to managing conflict is not figuring out how to manage the other person; the key to managing conflict is figuring out how to manage yourself.

- *Redefine success.* A conflict quickly can become a test of wills. For those who experienced childhood abuse, who so often felt as though they were the loser in conflicts, the desire to win can be very strong. But win-lose is not always the only outcome in conflicts. Often, a conscious effort can produce what is called a win-win. Because of how you grew up, the only model for conflict resolution you may have stems from when your abuser won and you lost. However, conflict resolution encompasses so much more than that. Healthy conflict resolution happens when both parties are able to present their needs and negotiate to find a solution that works for both of them.

- *Face forward.* Because of their history of abuse, a person may think avoidance is the only way to deal with conflict. They may try to evade conflict by pretending it doesn't exist or give up temporarily. In my experience, conflict doesn't go away. It comes to a head one way or another. My advice is to face forward and deal with the conflict. Working through it will not be particularly easy, but it is necessary.

- *Set the ground rules and stick to them.* Be clear on what you will and will not accept as you work through the conflict. Do not overlook abusive behavior or engage in abusive behavior yourself. One of the ground rules may be a cooling-off period that either party can call.

- *Factor in forgiveness.* Conflicts are difficult, and people can become overwhelmed with emotions. They can make mistakes in what they say and do. As a caveat—a mistake is not an intentional act of harm. But people can and will do things they regret in the heat of the moment. In that moment, when the person asks for forgiveness, grant it and then return to the issue at hand. In that moment, ask for forgiveness yourself and then return to the issue at hand. So many arguments I've witnessed between people have gotten completely sidetracked by these heat-of-the-moment words and actions. Instead of concentrating on the main issue, the two people skitter off into endless side issues that derail the main objectives.

- *Leave the salt in the shaker.* Do you know the expression "Pouring salt on a wound"? When working through a conflict, my advice is to leave the salt in the shaker and far away from any open wound. This is especially true for people who know each other well. Defensiveness may seem like a smart idea in conflict, but it only produces additional hostility and the temptation to retaliate—to get under the guard of the other person and inflict maximum damage. If the goal is to vanquish an enemy, this strategy makes sense. But ask yourself, is this person really my enemy?

- *Keep the goal in sight.* The goal in conflict is to, whenever possible, find a solution that works for both parties. If you can keep your sights firmly set on this goal, you can maintain a more positive, hopeful attitude through the roughness of the conflict itself. If you expect resolution, you may find resolution is easier to find.

- *Be focused but don't force.* The goal is to be consistent in your efforts to produce a resolution without attempting to force a predetermined outcome. The other person may say yes but mean no and have no real intention of following through, which will lead to further conflict.

- *Be clear with your goals.* Have you ever had an employer or teacher say to you, "Don't just bring me the problem, bring me the solution?" When in conflict with another person, be clear not only about what you believe is the problem but also what the solution or solutions might be. In this way, you create a starting point for resolution.

- *Watch yourself and the other person.* Remember, the goal isn't to win over or vanquish your opponent. Instead, you want to achieve a mutually agreed on resolution, which requires cooperation and negotiation. Sometimes in conflict, however, neither cooperation nor negotiation is possible. People can become emotionally overwhelmed; they can misunderstand an issue or perspective; they can even become physically exhausted. Each of these conditions can derail resolution. Not all conflicts must be resolved immediately. Some negotiations need to take place over a span of time. If either you or the other person becomes unable to continue, agree to pause and pick a time to reconvene. Allow for a break, a time-out, a cease-fire, a truce. Then use that time to compose yourself, review the positive work you've already done, and recommit to positive work to bring about full resolution when you've agreed to meet again.

One Step at a Time

When Doug first started counseling, he was an expert at beating himself up. He was unbelievably quick at finding fault with who he was and what he did. As quick as he was to find fault, he expected a similar velocity at finding a fix. When he made the same mistake twice, and three times, he would skirt the edge of despair and question what good it was to continue our work together.

At first, my job was to point out Doug's progress because he had not yet developed the skills to see it. Doug's internal compass was so set to the negative; he was blinded to anything positive. His recalibration happened through weekly visits for months, and it was not easy. I remember at least three times when he called and canceled all his appointments. I would convince him to come in, just one more time, for "closure," and then use that visit as a way to help him recalibrate.

The rapport I established with Doug helped him come to better understand both his relationship with others and, first and foremost, his relationship with himself. To help give him a visual for his recovery, I went online and showed him before-and-after pictures of natural disasters. We viewed several scenes of flooding and tornadoes. In each case, I would ask him if the person standing in front of their ruined home was responsible for either the rising waters or the gale-force winds. At first, Doug was reluctant to absolve the people of any responsibility. He would bring up flood plains and construction values. I would ask again if the people were responsible for the waters or the winds. He finally had to admit, no, they were not.

"You weren't responsible for your abuse either," I told him. "Your parents flooded you with negativity and knocked you over with their hatred toward each other. You were just a child and had no way to defend yourself."

I showed him the pictures of the destruction again and said, "Given the weather, was it any wonder the damage?" Doug, again, had to admit, no. I asked him, then, why would he be surprised to find damage in his own life. He responded by asking if I thought he was a wreck.

To answer, I went to the "after" pictures. We talked about the work, energy, and optimism that goes into rebuilding after a natural disaster. I explained that those were the very components needed to rebuild after a disastrous childhood. I asked him to look at the people in the "after" pictures and assign them probable characteristics. He said words such as *tough*, *proud*, *capable*, and *resourceful*. I told him I found him to possess those very same characteristics, which he could put to work in his own rebuilding.

Together we settled on a visual for his counseling; we were working on a Doug "remodel." He didn't want to tear down everything about his childhood but recognized the areas that needed considerable updating, as far as attitude and perspective were concerned. This analogy helped Doug be more patient with himself. As a do-it-yourselfer, he was extremely familiar with having to go back to the plumbing or electrical section multiple times until he found just the right fitting or fixture that would do the job. He had to concede that installing a new attitude could be even more complicated than installing a new toilet.

I hope you give yourself the time to rebuild your own relationships. In my experience, you must allow yourself the time to accomplish your goals, as well as the willingness to persevere through obstacles. You will need to accept the proverbial two steps forward and one step back.

I also believe you'll need one more vital thing to experience meaningful and lasting recovery. I've saved that one more thing for the final chapter. Many people, like Doug, have asked me a variation on these questions during their recovery: "How can I forgive? How can I heal and move on with my life?"

The answers to those questions come from different sources. The counseling relationship can hold answers. The personal stamina and fortitude of the individual can hold answers. The family and personal support systems can hold answers. But when those answers aren't enough, when the destruction of childhood abuse overwhelms a person, where can that person turn? I believe the power to restore and recover lies in the divine, redemptive power of love. I have seen the power of faith and spiritual belief provide the answers to overwhelming questions.

12

Steps to Spiritual Healing

"Why didn't God protect me? Why did he let this happen?" These are the devastatingly personal equivalents of the age-old question, "Why do bad things happen to good people?" and its mirror image, "Why do good things happen to bad people?" These questions touch at the heart of our stubborn sense that life should be fair, even in the face of overwhelming evidence that it is not. A person who has been abused as a child can come to substitute God for life in that sentence and conclude God wasn't or isn't fair.

If you grew up in a faith environment, where God was portrayed as all-knowing and all-loving, the thought that God isn't fair can seem heretical. God must be good and right, so the "fault," then, lies with you. When you were told you were unlovable, wrong, stupid, or worthless, those judgments were presented as coming from God and must, therefore, be correct. You conclude that because of your faults, God didn't find you worth protecting. He didn't consider you worthy of saving. Such twisted beliefs cause hope to strangle and die.

My practice, over the years, has come to be about resuscitating hope. In an earlier chapter, I gave examples of the types of spiritual implication I've seen:

- Some abused children understand God as their only refuge amid the abuse. They cling to God and credit him for saving them during their fragile childhood. Their relationship with God is strong.

- Other abused children are suspicious of God. This negativity is not always overt but may be subtle, a refusal to engage God to any great depth or degree. Their relationship with God is shallow.

- Some abused children are openly angry at God. They accept that God is all-knowing and all-powerful and, within that context, believe God knew what was happening to them and failed to protect them. They blame their abuser, but they also blame God. Their relationship with God is hostile.

- Other abused children are afraid of God. They believe in their total unworthiness and seek to please God, while also believing they can never succeed. Yet just as they tried to please their abuser to no avail, they continue to attempt to please God. Their relationship with God is fearful.

I suppose a person could have a completely indifferent view of God, and perhaps, this may happen more frequently now that we have entered a post-Christian culture.[1] However, my experience is that someone with an adult indifference to God often did not start out that way. Their childlike faith was drained from them, year after year, circumstance after circumstance, disappointment after disappointment. Rather than continue to have faith and be disappointed, they decided just to settle for life's disappointments, without faith. But a life without faith, a life indifferent to God, does not provide the spiritual answers I firmly believe are essential to long-term recovery from childhood abuse.

Hope Resuscitation

Do you have an indifferent view of God, a view you wouldn't even call faith? Do you remember always feeling that way? Was there a point in your life when you gave up on God and just decided he wasn't all that relevant to your life? If so, has something or someone else filled that void of belief? What do you firmly believe in now? What do you firmly rely on now to get through each day? Are those things a net positive or a net negative in your life?

Are you afraid of God? Do you want to be near God but feel you don't really belong there? Do you avoid getting close to God because you're afraid if he notices you, he will reject you?

Are you angry at God? Are you angry at what happened to you and the pain you suffered? Do you think God either doesn't care about you or meant for you to suffer? Have you decided that since God didn't care about you, you have no intention of caring about God?

Are you drawn to faith in God but aren't sure you can trust him? Are you confused about the role God played in the abuse you suffered? Are you worried that if you get closer to God, he will turn out to be like your abuser?

In these scenarios, each person determines something about who God is, based on what they have heard, seen, read, or experienced. If you hold one of these views of God, I'd like you to consider that your view may be warped. Even if you consider your faith in God to be strong, if you have weathered the storms of childhood abuse with your beliefs firmly intact, I still think a fresh look at God is a valuable endeavor. I believe a fresh look at God can resuscitate hope—and hope resuscitated can bring a fresh breath of faith.

Finding God

I've found one of the strongest components in resuscitating hope is letting God speak for himself. This is especially true if your childhood abuse was couched in spiritual or religious terms or if God was made out to be a silent partner, passing judgment from on high about the righteousness of your abuse. Your abuser acted as God's interpreter. Isn't it time to let God speak for himself?

A starting place to allow God to speak for himself is to read his Word. People have been reading the Bible for thousands of years, finding God's truth and character revealed within its pages. God's purpose for the Bible is for people to read it, yet I'm surprised by how many people don't. If you wanted to really know about someone and had an opportunity to read that person's personal journal, which revealed what they did, how they thought, and the values they held, wouldn't you jump at the chance? The Bible has been called God's love letter to humankind.

Can the Bible be hard to understand? Absolutely. But faith doesn't require perfect understanding. Hebrews 11:1 says that "faith is the confidence in what we hope for and assurance about what we do not see." Sometimes when I'm studying the Bible, I need faith that someday I'll truly understand the passages I am reading. When I need to wrestle with a difficult passage of Scripture or an elusive spiritual concept, I have learned to accept that challenge of waiting on understanding. I don't need to be perfect in my *understanding of God* to be able to *understand God*.

When I'm stuck, I go to James 1:5 for encouragement, "If any of you lacks wisdom, you should ask God, who gives generously to all without finding fault, and it will be given to you." Those of you who have been abused as children may find this passage hard to believe. You may totally understand the "lacks wisdom" part if you were told how stupid or incompetent you were growing up; your trouble may be with the rest of the verse. You may have

172

grown up avoiding asking for what you really wanted because of the response you knew you'd get. You may have been told God doesn't really care about you, so why bother to ask. You may have no experience with someone in authority giving generously and without assigning fault. If you grew up suspicious or disdainful of promises, you may react to the statement "and it will be given to you" with "yeah, right."

Reading the Bible and allowing God to speak for himself may not be easy. However, if you've gotten your concepts and ideas of God and faith through the filter of your abuser or your abuse, an unfiltered view of God's Word would be spiritually beneficial. You may ask, however, "How can I read the Bible unfiltered when what I read still comes through me? How can God be unfiltered when I'm always in the way?"

As a Christian, I don't believe I am on my own when it comes to understanding God or the Bible, though sometimes it can feel that way. When Jesus left this earth to return to God, he paved the way for the Holy Spirit to be our guide (see John 16:12–15). We have divine help, help we need to acknowledge and utilize. We're not supposed to try to figure out God all on our own.

To think otherwise is to fall into the trap of perfectionism. Some people distance themselves from God because they think they can only come to God when they are "perfect." A person who has undergone childhood abuse may feel the need to "clean up" before trying to approach God. However, because of the shame they carry, they never feel clean and, thus, avoid approaching God.

Finding Prayer

Just as reading God's Word is a wonderful way to get to know him, so is talking with God. You'll notice I didn't say talking to God. According to research, more than half of Americans say they pray every day,[2] but I have to wonder whether people are talking *to* God or *with* God. Talking to God is like a small child crawling up on Santa's lap at the mall and reciting the list of "I wants." Does God want to hear what we want? Yes! But I believe God has more in mind for prayer than hearing what he already knows (see Matt. 6:32). Through prayer, God wants to hear you, but I also believe God wants you to hear him. Two people talking with and hearing each other is a conversation, which is the best way to pray.

In prayer, sometimes God's voice is best heard in silence (see Ps. 46:10) or as a whisper (see 1 Kings 19:11–13). And, sometimes, God doesn't answer right away. Is this because he isn't prepared to give you an answer? No, I think this is because sometimes we're not yet prepared to hear his answer.

Because of the intimacy involved, talking with God can be an excruciating experience for those who have suffered childhood abuse. Those who have been abused may have learned to hide, to shield, to avoid, to close up tightly, or not to share out of fear. Prayer is an opening up of the heart, mind, and soul—an experience that can be terrifying.

I remember confidently telling a young woman who was abused as a child that I thought God already knew what she was thinking, so why not talk to him? Her answer humbled me. She said her abuser was skillful at knowing exactly how she was feeling and would use that knowledge against her, to belittle her, to demonstrate his power over her, to create feelings of hopelessness. When she put it that way, I understood why she was so fearful of prayer.

Given that reality, I suggested she find a prayer partner, perhaps an older female who she knew and trusted. She found a woman from her faith community who was in her eighties. This elderly woman had the time to devote to teaching this younger woman how to pray, praying with and for her until she was able to pray for herself.

Too often, those who have survived childhood abuse think they need to do everything on their own and hide what they consider to be their "failed" efforts. These beliefs bleed into all aspects of their lives, including the spiritual. All of us have spiritual resources, however, we can draw on to get the help we need and to obtain the wisdom God generously wants to give us, without once finding fault.

Finding Trust

Proverbs 3:5–6 says to "trust in the LORD with all your heart and lean not on your own understanding; in all your ways submit to him, and he will make your paths straight." How can you wholeheartedly embrace this challenge?

Do you remember the movie *Indiana Jones and the Last Crusade*? In my favorite scene from that movie, Indy must find a way to traverse a huge crevasse so he can save his dying father. Looking out over this bottomless pit, he knows there must be a way across but he cannot see it. Drawing a deep breath, he steps out into the abyss, taking a leap of faith. Doing so, his feet touch a narrow stone bridge, hidden optically by the surrounding rock. He reaches the other side, finds the Holy Grail, and saves his father.

In some ways, I think trust in God is like that. We know we need to trust—for our benefit or the benefit of others—but all we see is a bottomless pit of fear. It is a huge request to ask someone who has been abused, whose trust has been turned into a weapon against them, to trust despite everything they see. Yet Indy knew the bridge was there only because he stepped out into the abyss. What about you? How can you develop the trust unless you take that first step?

Trust comes through relationship. By reading the Bible and engaging with God in prayer, you will develop a relationship with him. Trusting him will become more comfortable the more you get to know him. I advise you to give yourself time. Learn who God is and how he works, which isn't like me or you (see Isa. 55:8). As you get to know God better, you'll be better at watching for the ways God is and has been trustworthy in your life.

Start with small acts of faith and trust. When you don't understand what God is doing, talk with him about how you feel. If you're not sure what to say, read through the psalms of David, who could be surprisingly honest with God about his fears and disappointments. Use David's words to articulate your frustrations and concerns.

Finding Forgiveness

For Thomas, forgiving his father was a step of faith that went too far. Thomas told me his father didn't deserve to be forgiven, not with what he had done. He stood solidly planted on the side of anger, looking across that abyss to forgiveness but refusing to cross.

From a personal point of view, I couldn't blame him. If I put myself in his shoes, I'd be hard-pressed to forgive too. But from a professional point of view, I knew how important forgiveness is. I've seen the transformative power of forgiveness at work.

I am privileged to see how forgiveness transforms the person doing the forgiving. Sometimes I also get to see how forgiveness transforms the person being forgiven, but not always. Sometimes the person to be forgiven is dead. Other times that person has left the relationship and is no longer accessible. Still other times that person is not safe and cannot remain in relationship. Forgiveness is still possible, though, because forgiveness is an action of the forgiver, whether it is ever received by the other person.

The Bible talks about forgiveness quite a lot. In Jesus's prayer in Matthew 6, as he's teaching the disciples how to pray, his example includes asking God to "forgive us our debts, as we also have forgiven our debtors" (v. 12). This pattern provides no qualification about whether the person even knows about your forgiveness or in any way deserves to be forgiven. All that is required is that you are aware of a debt someone owes you and you choose to forgive that person, in the same way you're asking God to forgive you. In many ways, that is a tough standard to meet.

But what about Thomas's objection? What about the truly wicked, for that is how Thomas saw his father. Thomas, who knew the Bible, talked about God's vengeance, wrath, and judgment. I had to acknowledge those aspects of God's character, but I needed Thomas to consider there was more to God than "fire and brimstone."

Thomas's father had died almost a year before he came in to see me. I asked him if he'd inherited any family photos from the estate. I remember him looking extremely puzzled when I asked him to bring in as many family photos as he could to our next appointment, including any he had of his father as a child.

I wasn't sure if Thomas would follow through, but he did. He arrived at our next appointment with a small box of pictures, some yellowed and fraying with age. We took a few minutes to go through them, as Thomas told me what he could remember or had been told about each one. We had to laugh at some of the outrageous clothes and hairstyles from the past.

Then Thomas lifted out of the box a small black-and-white photo of his father as a child. It must have been around seventy years old. In the picture, his father was standing with a collared shirt, suspenders, and short pants. He wasn't smiling.

I asked Thomas what he saw in that picture. He didn't say much beyond mentioning that he never knew his father to smile much, even as an adult. I asked Thomas to consider that God looked at that picture, at that boy, and saw something more. I asked Thomas to consider that God saw his father as someone precious.

I still wasn't getting much reaction out of Thomas, so I asked him what he thought God wanted for the boy in the picture. Thomas said he thought God would probably have wanted that boy to turn out to be a better man. I told Thomas I agreed and reminded him that God's plan was never for his father to turn out the way he did. We talked about missed chances and bad choices and how those choices can have such terrible effects. Thomas still couldn't wrap his mind around forgiveness. "What good will it do to forgive him?" he asked. "He's dead."

"But you're not," I replied. "Forgiveness isn't for him; forgiveness is for you."

Thomas still wasn't sold, so I asked him to leave that little picture of his father out where he could see it over the next week. I also asked him to think about how much time and energy he'd spent being angry, resentful, and bitter about his father since he came of age himself. I already knew it was considerable; unresolved anger was one reason he was seeing me.

When Thomas came back for the next appointment, he was much more thoughtful, less reactive. He wanted a solid reason for forgiving his father when his father didn't deserve it. I told him that even people who didn't deserve to be forgiven could be. When he asked me for proof, I explained the example of Jesus as he was dying on the cross. With his last breaths of life, Jesus asked God to forgive the very people who were putting him to death. Forgiveness, I told Thomas, is one of the foundational aspects of God's character. I also reminded Thomas of God's words from Ezekiel, where God says he doesn't take pleasure in the death of anyone (see Ezek. 18:32). Thomas wanted to hate the boy in the picture; God wanted to love him.

Thomas said his father never shared much about his own life growing up or what he'd had to endure. I asked Thomas to consider that someone, somewhere, had probably hurt that little boy in the picture, maybe in similar ways that little boy had grown up to hurt Thomas. I offered up forgiveness to break that cycle. I suggested to Thomas that the only way to move on with his life and to truly let his father go was to forgive him.

Thomas's questions about forgiveness have been echoed by many others. Why would Jesus forgive? Why doesn't God take pleasure in the death of the wicked (see Ezek. 18:23)? The answer I have come to believe in is because of love. I truly believe God shows us examples of forgiveness because he wants us to learn how to forgive.

Yet, forgiveness can appear at war with justice. Thomas was reluctant to forgive because he believed doing so would let his father off the hook. I told him I thought God was very much aware of what his father had done, because nothing is secret from God (see Heb. 4:13). God knows yet chooses to forgive because of his love.

Forgiveness is truly a blessing from God. It blesses the one forgiven but it also blesses the one who forgives. Those able to find the strength to forgive come to understand this foundational aspect of God's character.

Who do you keep tied around your neck by an unforgiving chain? Who would you like to be free from? Who would you like to forgive so you can move forward with your life and your relationships? Forgiveness doesn't seem to make any more sense than stepping off the edge of an abyss. Yet it might be the only way to save a life—you or someone else.

Finding Truth

Understanding who God is creates the foundation for restoring hope. Understanding who God is also helps you understand who you are. The abuse you suffered taught you lies about who you are. God wants you to know the truth. Do you remember the section in

179

this book on cognitive dissonance and the ways childhood abuse can warp the truth? Below are the examples I gave, along with a verse that comes to my mind for each. I encourage you, as you read God's Word and spend time in conversation with him, to find God's words of truth and make them your own. When you find these words of truth, write them down, memorize them, and use them to counter the lies you've been told and the lies you were forced to live.

You are not stupid. "If any of you lacks wisdom, you should ask God, who gives generously to all without finding fault, and it will be given to you" (James 1:5).

You are not in danger. "The LORD is my shepherd, I lack nothing. He makes me lie down in green pastures, he leads me beside quiet waters, he restores my soul" (Ps. 23:1).

You are not worthless. "For you know that it was not with perishable things such as silver or gold that you were redeemed from the empty way of life handed down to you from your ancestors, but with the precious blood of Christ, a lamb without blemish or defect" (1 Pet. 1:18–19).

You are not unlovable. "For God so loved the world that he gave his one and only Son, that whoever believes in him shall not perish but have eternal life" (John 3:16).

You are not doomed to fail. "For we are God's handiwork, created in Christ Jesus to do good works, which God prepared in advance for us to do" (Eph. 2:10).

You are not destined to stay a victim. "No, in all these things we are more than conquerors through him who loved us" (Rom. 8:37).

You are more than a victim of your childhood abuse; you are more than a conqueror through the power of God. You can conquer your past and integrate that past victoriously into the present and future. Impossible, you say? Remember Matthew 19:26, "Jesus looked at them and said, 'With man this is impossible, but with God all things are possible.'"

The whole-person approach to healing includes spirituality and faith for a reason. Recovery, reconciliation, and resuscitation often fall into the category of a miracle because they require the impossibility of God. Thomas thought he would have to live with his anger over his father for the rest of his life, poisoning his relationships and sabotaging his health. He thought forgiving his father was impossible—until he stepped off his anger and into the abyss of faith, where he found God's bridge of forgiveness waiting for him.

The Journey to Recovery

Thomas didn't find his way to forgiveness on his own. He had help. You aren't required to take this journey by yourself, either. You can get help. If you're able, consider obtaining professional counseling. Seek out competent, spiritual counsel through your faith community. Find trustworthy friends and family who can support you to reach your goals. Continue to study and read books that speak to you and assist you in filling in the gaps you find as you continue.

May God bless your journey to recovery from the pain you have endured. The road is long and arduous, but the destination is glorious. When you are weary of walking, take one more step. When you think you're at your darkest point, remember, to God, evening is always followed by morning (see Gen. 1:3).

My prayer is that you will reclaim or renew your childlike faith, the faith that Jesus said leads to the kingdom of God. This kingdom is the pearl of great price. Do you remember the parable Jesus told in Matthew 13:44? "The kingdom of heaven is like treasure hidden in a field. When a man found it, he hid it again, and then in his joy went and sold all he had and bought that field." To secure that treasure, God may be asking you to sell all you have, including your anger and shame, your fears and anxieties, your insecurities and perfectionism, and your unforgiveness.

Have courage and find hope. Find hope in the things you can't see right now. Have faith in the impossible things God causes to happen every day.

Notes

Chapter 1 The Hide-and-Seek of Childhood Abuse

1. Matthew 19:14.
2. Matthew 19:26.

Chapter 2 Not Normal but Too Common

1. Michael Eric Dyson, "Punishment or Child Abuse?" *New York Times*, September 17, 2014, http://www.nytimes.com/2014/09/18/opinion/punishment -or-child-abuse.html? r=0.

Chapter 5 The Violation of Neglect and Physical and Sexual Abuse

1. *Dictionary.com*, s.v. "neglect," accessed January 10, 2017, http://www.dictionary .com/browse/neglect?s=t.
2. "When Did It Become a Legal Requirement to Wear Seat Belts?" Reference. com, accessed January 10, 2017, https://www.reference.com/government-politics /did-become-legal-requirement-wear-seat-belts-fe742a43c9703cdb.
3. Diane DePanfilis, *Child Neglect: A Guide for Prevention, Assessment, and Intervention* (US Department of Health and Human Services, 2006), 9–19, https:// www.childwelfare.gov/pubPDFs/neglect.pdf#page=11&view=Chapter 2 Definition and Scope of Neglect.
4. "Raising Awareness about Sexual Abuse," National Sex Offender Public Website, accessed January 11, 2017, https://www.nsopw.gov/(X(1)S(pdmy0slrj tvpkwqavn5d2how))/en/Education/FactsStatistics?AspxAutoDetectCookieSup port=1#victims.

Chapter 7 Additional Costs of Childhood Abuse

1. University of California–Los Angeles Health Sciences, "Abuse, Lack of Parental Warmth in Childhood Linked to Multiple Health Risks in Adults,"

Science Daily, accessed January 12, 2017, https://www.sciencedaily.com/releases /2013/09/130926205005.htm.

2. "Stress Effect on the Body," American Psychological Association, accessed January 12, 2017, http://www.apa.org/helpcenter/stress-body.aspx.

3. Matthew 18:6.

Chapter 8 Steps to Emotional Healing

1. *Wikipedia*, s.v., "self-fulfilling prophecy," accessed January 13, 2016, https:// en.wikipedia.org/wiki/Self-fulfilling_prophecy.

Chapter 9 Steps to Cognitive Healing

1. Felicia Gould et al., "The Effects of Childhood Abuse and Neglect on Cognitive Functioning in Adulthood," *Journal of Psychiatric Research* 46, no. 4 (2012): 500–06, http://www.journalofpsychiatricresearch.com/article/S0022-3956(12)00006-4 /abstract; Valentina Nikulina and Cathy Spatz Widom, "Child Maltreatment and Executive Functioning in Middle Adulthood: A Prospective Examination," *Neuropsychology* 27, no. 4 (July 2013): 417–27, http://www.ncbi.nlm.nih.gov/pub med/23876115; Matthias Majer et al., "Association of Childhood Trauma with Cognitive Function in Healthy Adults: A Pilot Study," *BMC Neurology* (July 2010), http://www.ncbi.nlm.nih.gov/pubmed/20630071.

Chapter 10 Steps to Physical Healing

1. "What Is Healthy Sleep?" National Sleep Foundation, accessed February 16, 2017, https://sleepfoundation.org/shift-work/content/what-healthy-sleep.

2. Mayo Clinic, "Nearly Seven in Ten Americans Take Prescription Drugs, Mayo Clinic, Olmsted Medical Center Find," news release, June 19, 2013, http://news network.mayoclinic.org/discussion/nearly-7-in-10-americans-take-prescription -drugs-mayo-clinic-olmsted-medical-center-find/.

Chapter 12 Steps to Spiritual Healing

1. Jeremy Weber, "15 Measurements of Whether Americans Are Post-Christian (Infographic)," *Christianity Today*, April 15, 2013, http://www.christianitytoday .com/gleanings/2013/april/15-measurements-of-whether-americans-are-post -christian.html.

2. Michael Lipka, "5 Facts about Prayer," Pew Research Center, May 4, 2016, http://www.pewresearch.org/fact-tank/2016/05/04/5-facts-about-prayer/.

Gregory L. Jantz, PhD, is a popular speaker and award-winning author of more than twenty-five books, including *Healing the Scars of Emotional Abuse* and *Every Woman's Guide to Managing Your Anger*. He is the founder of The Center for Counseling & Health Resources, Inc. (www.aplaceofhope.com) in the state of Washington.

Ann McMurray has partnered with Dr. Jantz for twenty-five years, both in writing collaboration and at The Center • A Place of Hope, where she is operations manager.

Hope and healing
for the victims
of emotional abuse

You can live free from anxiety

With compassion, common sense, and biblical wisdom, Dr. Jantz will help you identify the causes of your anxiety, assess the severity of your symptoms, and start down avenues for positive change.

Do you feel
STUCK AND UNFULFILLED
in your relationships?

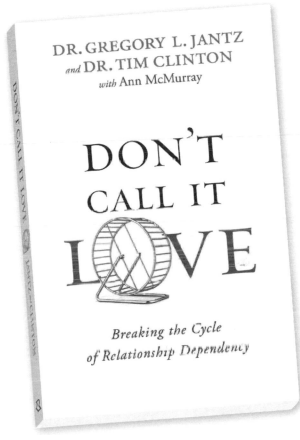

In a warm, engaging style, Drs. Jantz and Clinton help you unravel why you're drawn back to the same types of people and relationships over and over again. You'll learn how to break the cycle of relationship dependency, focus on finding wholeness as a unique individual, and discover the key to finding a healthy relationship that lasts.